I knew I would like this book from the moment I read that Amanda had inherited a loathing of filing! This is a must-read for all perfectionists who struggle with the desire for tidy, clutter-free lives and homes, and yet face daily the guilt of things not done and the mess of existing in a fallen world. Using humour, apt teaching from Scripture and loads of practical advice (including some great recipes!), Amanda, in this hugely encouraging book, shows how God in his grace and providence is able to help us, despite all our imperfections, to be organized enough to focus on what really matters: serving Christ and all the people he has given us to love.
Tricia Marnham, Bible teacher and former solicitor

This book takes an honest, realistic and humorous look at the common misconception that ministry and perfection are somehow synonymous. *The Ministry of a Messy House* reminds us that we are actually far messier than we realize, but our perfect Saviour delights to work through us for his glory.
Jane McNabb, minister's wife, conference speaker and author

We can't escape mess. However organized we are, the laundry is never done, the children aren't clean for long, church relationships are often frayed and our hearts are messed up with sin. Shot through with practical resources and biblical truth, this book reminds us with refreshing honesty how God wants to tackle the mess in our hearts. And the rest of the mess? He'll use it to display his grace, and teach us to trust him and reveal him to others. Highly recommended!
Elizabeth McQuoid, author of The Amazing Cross *and* The Transforming Trinity

Encouraging, practical, humorous and warm: this book is a gem and a wonderful affirmation of the grace of Christ that works in, and not despite, our mess.
Emma Scrivener, writer and speaker

I spend a lot of time dreaming about being a godly domestic success, as I gaze on the chaos that is my life. I know I'm saved by grace alone, by faith alone, but I have a sneaking suspicion that God will think more highly of me if my house is tidy, my cooking divine and my children are kitted out

in Boden (ironed). Amanda's book offers me hope in my hopeless pursuit of domestic perfection. Her distillation of scriptural wisdom, front-line experience as a busy vicar's wife and mum, practical advice and sense of humour will help all of us failed domestic goddesses to trust in a sovereign God, who works not despite of, but through, the mess of our lives, while challenging those who maybe have made their perfect home their idol.

Now, where did I put my copy . . . ?

Lizzy Smallwood, minister's wife, mum, speaker and author

the Ministry of
a Messy House

The Ministry of a Messy House

Grace in place of guilt

Amanda Robbie

INTER-VARSITY PRESS
Norton Street, Nottingham NG7 3HR, England
Email: ivp@ivpbooks.com
Website: www.ivpbooks.com

First published 2013

British Library Cataloguing in Publication Data
A catalogue record for this book is available from the British Library.

ISBN: 978–1–78359–005–6
ePub: 978–1–78359–036–0
Mobi: 978–1–78359–037–7

Set in Dante 12/15pt
Typeset in Great Britain by CRB Associates, Potterhanworth, Lincolnshire
Printed in Great Britain by Ashford Colour Press Ltd, Gosport, Hampshire

Inter-Varsity Press publishes Christian books that are true to the Bible and that communicate the gospel, develop discipleship and strengthen the church for its mission in the world.

Inter-Varsity Press is closely linked with the Universities and Colleges Christian Fellowship, a student movement connecting Christian Unions in universities and colleges throughout Great Britain, and a member movement of the International Fellowship of Evangelical Students. Website: www.uccf.org.uk

For Neil
who's great with all the mess

Contents

Acknowledgments

I wasn't actually planning to write a book, but here we are. Printed on paper and everything. So my very grateful thanks go to everyone who's helped me get here:

- My ace husband, Neil, who has carried even more than his usually large share of family duties whilst I've been writing, alongside the more-than-full-time job of being a vicar. He's lived through, and with, all the mess for a good few years now and still has the grace to be patient with me.
- My lovely messy kids, Isha, Gillis and Elliot, who have supplied book illustrations over and above the call of duty. I'm sorry about the lack of socks, especially on Monday mornings.
- My mum, who badgered me into starting my blog, *The Vicar's Wife*, and is unflaggingly supportive and encouraging. The blog was the reason why I was asked to speak at the Midlands Women's Convention (only for three minutes, mind), which was how I got asked to write this book. And to my dad, who wrote the great poem at the beginning of the book and seems to have passed on to me both his excellent journalistic instincts and a variety of messy tendencies, including a deep loathing of filing. Also my brilliant mother-in-law, Meg, who is the Sir Edmund Hillary of vicarage laundry mountains and indefatigable provider of food and welcome to all comers. And my sister, Josie, who models a firm trust in God's grace and providence (and spotted a wobbly chapter ending for me

after an all-night read-through), and all my extended family, who've been cheering me on and who graciously put up with the mess when they visit and are very understanding about belated birthday cards.

- Ros, who has found time in the midst of writing her PhD and a few novels and working for a church to give me much-valued first-cut editorial advice and many happy distractions on Twitter. She is a great model of messy hospitality.
- Our long-suffering ministry trainee lodgers: Tommy, Simon (and Kim), Luke and the recently arrived Jon, who've been part of our messy-house ministry here in West Bromwich. Thank you for sharing our lives and the gospel here in the mess. A special mention to Janette, who cleans the vicarage every couple of weeks and is never fazed by the mess. Also our Families and Community Worker, Helen, who joined us in the parish just before I started writing and has brought patience and good humour and great wisdom on messy families.
- Eleanor, my patient editor, who always looks immaculate but recommends putting creased clothes under a mattress in preference to ironing. Only when under pressure, mind. And Ian Mitchell for the superb illustrations. I think he may have set up a surveillance camera in the vicarage.
- Our lovely church family at Holy Trinity, who join us in, and help us through, the mess in so many ways. And everyone who prayed or supplied stories and ideas in person, on the blog or on social media. I have been encouraged on my way by many other messy Christians who cling to God's grace and trust his providence in their lives.

Messiness

Some live their lives, as can be seen,
Neat and efficient with a 'tidy' gene.
Not so the rest of us, who find
That things are lost or left behind.
We turn up slightly late, because
Somehow the cat's got muddy paws
Over the service sheets, and then,
Help, I've mislaid the keys again.
We dodge the papers stacked upon
The stairs, and hope they haven't gone,
Tidied away, Oh, here they are; who put them there?
(It may be me, I just don't care.)
But all among the piles of toys,
A muddy football – that's the boys –
The Christmas cards we didn't send,
There's always room to seat a friend,
Just one, but if there's even more,
Just move that pile onto the floor.
So, come and talk, some tea and cakes,
To love one's neighbour messy makes,
There's just no time to tidy up,
We always need another cup,
For family, friends and cruel distress
Come first, and so, you see,
A mess.

– John Turtle

Introduction: Messy me

White teeth, fancy cakes and bridal gowns. That's what Google thinks I'm after when I search for 'perfection'. Or if I'm after 'perfect', then the search engine assumes I want to make a crab linguine or perhaps compare my weekend with that of an Olympic cyclist or an actor. Being 'Perfectly Dressed' and 'Perfectly Elegant' in a 'Perfectly Designed' item of clothing is how Marks & Spencer have recently been trying to sell us their clothes.

Everywhere we are bombarded with messages telling us to seek perfection – in our looks, our homes and our lives in general. We might be told to do it by advertisers, or we may simply be comparing ourselves or our circumstances with others. We take the messages on board and we vaguely remember what Jesus told his followers: 'You therefore must be perfect, as your heavenly Father is perfect' (Matthew 5:48).

And then, we start to despair or just give up.

At the office or the school gate or at church, it seems that everyone else is almost perfect. And I'm not. She has so elegantly styled her hair this morning and all her data is ready for the meeting. I, by contrast, can barely see my desk and couldn't find my hairbrush as I ran out of the house. Her children are so well behaved and all toting vast pyramids constructed for the Ancient Egypt project. Mine are squabbling, and we've left the scribbled pictures of mummies on the dining room table. Other churches always have lively worship bands, not lousy CDs with the weird musical interlude in the middle of a song. And their preachers always stick to time and never forget their notes or get the names of the baptism candidates mixed up. Then I'm watching *MasterChef* and feeling depressed about my plan for sausages and mash for tea. Again. Perhaps I need to make an accompanying red wine *jus* and some Tuscan fries? I don't want to provide any mince pies for the church carol service – my pastry always turns out soggy and, unless I make my own, they just won't be good enough. Everyone else makes theirs from scratch, even the mincemeat, and their pies look ready to win the Star Baker award in *The Great British Bake Off*. Perfection is out there; it's just that I've not yet achieved it.

I only have to peek in my handbag to see that I am far from that ideal: alongside the essentials of purse, keys, phone and Filofax, I find an empty Maltesers packet and a small foil-wrapped chocolate egg left over from Easter. There are also some service sheets from last month, old sermon notes, a puzzle page torn from a newspaper a couple of weeks ago, an out-of-date voucher for a sports shop, details of half-term swimming sessions for kids and an already shopped-for shopping list. I also find my passport, which really ought to be safely filed away, and a pack of Happy Families cards that I bought for the kids last week and promptly forgot about.

perfection is out there; it's just that I've not yet achieved it.

My handbag is a messy mix of order and disorder – things I need and clutter that I don't – items essential for daily life and rubbish that should be headed straight for the bin. And it's not just my handbag. There is mess, both physical and relational, in every area of my life, and I seem to spend my time either sorting it out or thinking that I ought to be doing so. And when I talk to my friends, I find out that it's not just me, but there are many others struggling as I do. However much we clear out our handbags, cook perfect crab linguine and organize perfect weekends, we find that our homes, our churches, our communities and our relationships keep going awry.

And actually, we know that every other person on earth is a bit of a mess too, however well-hidden that mess may be. In truth, our cluttered lives reflect our disordered hearts. My heart is a spiritual mess, and that is why the rest of my life is less than perfect. But the good news is that we can live with our messy hearts in a messy world when we remember that we are children of a perfect and loving heavenly Father who knows our weaknesses: 'My grace is sufficient for you, for my power is made perfect in weakness' (2 Corinthians 12:9).

So be encouraged: it is through our messy lives that God's perfect power can be seen. His power can be seen when he brings good from our failures. It is seen when he changes our hearts. If I need to wield the hoover but can't bear the thought of it, he will give me strength. If I have an apologetic phone call to make and am fearful, his power is enough. If he wants to teach me about himself in a church service full of microphone feedback, his Spirit is able. If he is to bring us to heaven, he will not be thwarted by our clutter and our calamities. We don't need to be defeated by the mess. For he is sufficient.

He who calls you is faithful; he will surely do it.
(1 Thessalonians 5:24)

Amanda Robbie
May 2013

1. A perfect mess?

'Some people might find you a bit intimidating.'

I really can't think what gave my friend that idea. Well, apart from me being very loud, self-confident and bossy, that is. And quite tall. She'd told me how theological college was a community of saints – and also a community of sinners. And then she warned me that I should be careful how I came across. I appreciated her direct approach. I'm not very good at picking up on subtle hints.

My husband was soon to start training for Church of England ministry. We had spent an afternoon with these wise Christian friends who were already living on campus at the college we were headed for. Theological college can be a funny old place where relationships are often very intense. With people studying, worshipping and living together, you get to see one another in very sharp focus.

So, I arrived at college fully determined to restrain myself as much as possible. God clearly thought I'd be unable to do this unaided, so what actually happened when we started was that I contracted a horrible virus and was laid up in bed for about a month. No chance of being too scary then. Or so I hoped.

Later, when we'd settled in, I thought I'd check up on how I'd done with the not-being-frightening thing, so I asked a new friend about it. Did she think I was intimidating when she had first met me?

I'd not done as well as I thought because she replied, 'I did at first.' [Long pause.] 'But then I saw your house.' [Another pause, then laughter.]

The state of my campus house was indeed pretty cluttered. Well, more than cluttered. We had two adults, two small children, two cats and the contents of two houses in a small college home. And I never

do housework unless it's unavoidable (or there are other less attractive things to do), so it was only just on the right side of hygienic. Although my personality gives the impression that I'm totally on top of everything, my house reveals the truth. That I'm a mess.

Of course, not everyone has a house as messy as mine. Perhaps mess is limited to just a couple of old service sheets lurking in the bottom of a handbag or simply that drawer in the kitchen containing bits of string, old keys, batteries needing to be recharged and random metal widgets that look like they might be important. Maybe there is no physical clutter at all because it's all been sorted out – hooray! But, bad news, it will still need sorting out tomorrow or at some future date.

And the physical mess that we deal with every day – in our homes and our handbags, in the office or the garden, wherever – is just a reflection of the emotional and spiritual mess deep within our hearts and permeating our world. We can see that less tangible mess in all our relationships and in the world around us: family, house, church and life are never where they should be.

Contrast this with God's command: 'As he who called you is holy, you also be holy in all your conduct, since it is written, "You shall be holy, for I am holy"' (1 Peter 1:15–16).

If we're called to be holy, to be set apart for God, reflecting his perfect character, how then can we cope when our lives are far from holy and this is reflected in the less-than-perfect state of our houses and handbags, our churches and our communities? What is God doing in this mess that is my life? And how am I going to stay sane and godly when faced with a handbag full of sticky fluff, another pile of cat sick, yet another set of pyjamas left on the bathroom floor and the remains of an abandoned craft project that I've just found under the kitchen table?

What is mess?

Is mess just what happens in life? Or is it avoidable if we are organized/ holy/prayerful enough? If I keep everything under control, will my parents approve of my life choices? If I'm holy and pray a lot, will the kids stop bickering, and will my colleague respect me? Our New Year resolutions are often aimed at these messy areas of our lives: our tidiness, our uncontrolled eating or our tendency to sloth. But come February, the resolutions have been abandoned and once again we are submerged in clutter and cake crumbs. Books are available on tackling mess: managing my time, being a domestic goddess or some other such thing, and I've bought a few of them, even put some of the suggestions into practice, hoping that by reading them and changing the way I do things, the mess will disappear. But it hasn't.

Mess is not a Bible word, but sadly it is a by-product of sin, a problem affecting us all, dealt with right at the heart of the Bible. This means that mess cannot be totally avoided, no matter how many books of top tips we read or however much bleach we apply literally and metaphorically to our homes, our workplaces and our lives. We read in the opening chapters of Genesis how God made our world perfect, and how men and women were in perfect relationships with him and with one another. Then Eve met the snake, and she and Adam chose to doubt God's Word and believe the created serpent rather than the good Creator who had warned them not to eat the fruit of the tree of the knowledge of good and evil. But once she and her husband chose their own path and ate that fruit, our world began to fall apart. Mess has been with us ever since.

Mess can come to us through our own sin or that of others. Thus, my angry shouting at the kids is sin, of course, making a mess of our family relationships. Their fighting over whose turn it is to read the Bible in our family devotions (about which I have just shouted at them) is also sin and this too makes a mess of our relationships with one another. My frosty relationship with my neighbour may be due to their sin of not liking people with short haircuts or my sin of thoughtlessly having parked my car across their driveway once too often.

Mess can come to us through what we do (commission), like when we throw that plate at the wall in frustration, but also through what we fail to do (omission), like when we don't clear up the shards of crockery because we are still too cross. Often, I feel that my sins of omission weigh heavier on me. I can see so much that needs to be done, but don't have the time, nor the energy, nor the ability to do it. I have an imagination far greater than my personal capacity. Sometimes, it's hard to live with the thought of everything that needs to be done and my failure to carry it out.

Like Adam and Eve, we usually try to blame someone else for our mess – and the snake didn't have a leg to stand on. None of my children was ever responsible for the crayoning on the wall: 'Not me, Mummy'. It's never my fault that my daughter is yelling at me. These may seem like trivial things but they are real issues which offend God and damage his world and my relationships. I should not therefore treat them lightly. Nevertheless, at such times, I need to remember that, because of the death of Jesus in my place, because our God is rich in mercy towards me, I can be forgiven: for the frosty situation with the girl who used to be such a close friend, or for what I have failed to do – the call I didn't make to that sad friend, the hour that got squeezed out when I should have been preparing to lead home group.

Jesus came into our world to deal with our sin and its messy results. The cross at the centre of our faith on which he died was where he bore the punishment for our sins. The forgiveness bought there continues to be available to us throughout our lives. But often, we are so bogged down in the mess that we doubt God's goodness and his faithfulness to his promises. We don't believe that we are genuinely free from the condemnation we feel inside. We doubt that we are truly Christians and give way to despair, or at least apathy. At such times, God's grace is the remedy we need to apply – we need to seek and grasp hold of his gift of free unmerited favour towards us. And I will have strength to keep going if I understand the work of God's providence: his ordering of the world, including my failure, bringing about his good purposes for us and for the whole of creation.

Grace in the mess

Our messy lives, though inevitable in this world until Jesus returns in glory to wrap up time and reign over the new heavens and new earth, need not define us nor weigh us down. God's grace caused him to send us Jesus, thereby bringing us reconciliation with the Father, bought at the cross. And his grace doesn't just save us, but continues to enable us to live for him, so we can also offer grace to others in our dealings with them. What's more, that same grace keeps us for eternity. These three aspects of grace are highlighted in the chorus of the song 'Grace Unmeasured', by Bob Kauflin, which I try to sing to myself as often as possible:

> Grace paid for my sins
> And brought me to life
> Grace clothes me with power
> To do what is right
> Grace will lead me to heaven
> Where I'll see Your face
> And never cease
> To thank You for Your grace[1]

Saved by grace (grace paid for my sins)

If we look back to the beginning of our Christian journey, we can see that we had no idea that we needed God or his forgiveness. We were sinners, stuck in our personal mess, maybe even enjoying the chaos of a life without God. We may not have looked messy on the outside, because we were working hard to contain the heart mess. But it was still there, under the surface, ready to boil over when we least expected it.

Even if you were brought up in a Christian family and have never really known a time of unbelief, sin will not be an unfamiliar concept. Just join us in our vicarage on any morning as the day begins, Sundays especially, when the devil likes to ensure that we reach church in the worst of all possible moods. On a Sunday, everything that can go wrong is pretty much guaranteed to go completely pear-shaped. There may be no milk for the breakfast cereal (a regular sin of omission on my part), and then the children, with less structure to their morning, will find ways to niggle at one another. Alternatively, the kids will just fail to get dressed or eat breakfast, so that I descend into frantic and ungodly flapping and cajoling as I anticipate that, despite living right next door, we will be late for church. Again.

The apostle Paul knew what it was to have led a messy life before God's grace intervened. He even persecuted Christians before his dramatic conversion on the road to Damascus. In his letter to the believers in Ephesus, he writes about our incapacity to save ourselves, and how it is God's grace alone that saves us. This is a good place to start when we think about the mess in our lives. It's the difference between being dead and being alive:

> You were dead in the trespasses and sins in which you once walked, following the course of this world . . . But God, being rich in mercy . . . made us alive together with Christ . . . For by grace you have been saved through faith. And this is not your own doing; it is the gift of God, not a result of works, so that no one may boast. For we are his workmanship, created in Christ Jesus for good works, which God prepared beforehand, that we should walk in them.
> (Ephesians 2:1–10)

If we're Christians, we have experienced God's grace: he has opened our eyes to see the value of Christ's death for us. He has given us the gift of faith in him. And, by his Holy Spirit, his grace is continually available to us, even as we continue to return to dead ways while trying to walk in the good works prepared for us.

Kept by grace and in grace (grace clothes me with power)

So, God's grace has not only brought us to saving faith, but also keeps us going as Christians. That day when we missed the bus for work because we overslept due to watching utter rubbish on the telly the night before when we should have been going to bed? We can seek his grace. When I've snapped at the needy friend who called once again as I was trying to concentrate on preparing that Sunday school session? God is waiting for me to seek his grace. His grace is his gift to us in the daily mess of our lives. His grace is his favour towards us, while we are still sinners (Romans 5:8). Here and now he continues to work in me so I'm not alone in the continuing chaos of imperfect relationships and imperfect me.

I need to turn to God for help and I need to do it now. I need to look at the state of the boys' bedroom floor – honestly, how many small furry toys are necessary for a game to be enough fun? – and pray, not shout at them or turn away and head downstairs. I need God's grace so that I don't add to the mess. In fact, I can instead *show* God's grace as I continue to experience it. Remember, each experience of the mess of others is a grace opportunity: the colleague who hasn't delivered the document you needed, the coffee rota member who's cried off once again, the aged relative who wants you to sort out the gas supplier. When we feel inadequate, tired or just plain grumpy – a mess ourselves – we can remember that not only have we received grace, but God's grace is sufficient. In Paul's second letter to the Corinthians, he talks about how our weaknesses, our failures and omissions, enable God's power to be seen: 'But he [the Lord] said to me, "My grace is sufficient for you, for my power is made perfect in weakness." Therefore I will boast all the more gladly of my weaknesses, so that the power of Christ may rest upon me' (2 Corinthians 12:9).

God's forgiveness and mercy are available to us at all times and in all messes. We need to find ways to access this grace daily and hourly. I know deep down that the answer to nearly every problem in my Christian life is: 'pray and read the Bible'. I know I need to do these things if I am to trust God more and remember his grace. (Not that that makes it any easier, mind.)

Changes in circumstances may well mean that the devotional routine which was fine with the old commute to work is hopeless now that the office has moved, and the Bible reading notes which worked for me as a student are perhaps harder to engage with when time away from frantic activity seems to be available only in short slots. As my life has changed from single to married, and between different jobs, and more recently as my children have grown beyond toddlerhood, my Bible reading and prayer routines have changed frequently.

Sometimes, that change has been for the better and sometimes for the worse, but I keep trying to find a pattern that works for the season I am in.

It was a big shock to the family system just a few months ago when my daughter started secondary school. Suddenly, our day was beginning about an hour earlier, and my devotional routine wasn't working. Mornings are not my speciality, and I struggle even to think at all before breakfast, so just moving my old quiet time to an earlier slot wasn't going to cut it. It's taken a term to find a pattern for the family that works, but now this includes breakfast in bed for me and my daughter (fetched by me and brought back upstairs) an hour earlier when the vicarage is an hour colder. Then, I read and pray while she dresses and tries to get her act together. Once I've prayed, I'm able to help her to find all the lost items she still needs and usher her out of the door just in time for the usual bus, or possibly the one after that. In another year or so, my elder son will be at secondary school and the routine will need adapting once again.

Most years, I end up trying a new devotional book or Bible reading routine. This may not work for everyone, but as someone who quickly gets stale, I'm keen to try new approaches regularly. I may not read the devotional to the end, but if it's worth reading at all, it's likely to be worth reading until halfway through it. If dated notes fill me with guilt because of the unread days, I can always find an undated book. But if even a book seems too much to handle, a diary with a daily verse or an app on my phone is a way to hear God's Word, or I can use an audio Bible or listen to Christian music. I need to grab some of God's Word and take it with me and do this in a small way rather than not at all. I need to make sure above all else that I access the grace that 'clothes me with power'.

Kept for grace (grace will lead me to heaven)

But grace is not only something we can look back to, as we remember the cross, nor simply the daily sustenance for the Christian life. It is also what we are able to look forward to in each moment of the Christian life. God's promises will be fulfilled, mess will be gone, and so we can now live by faith in those promises, as John Piper so clearly describes in his book *Future Grace*: 'There is no saving act of faith – whether looking back to history, out to a person, or forward to a promise – that does not include a future orientation.'[2]

So we can look at the physical, emotional and relational mess, and its ultimate cause, the spiritual mess in our hearts, and recognize that it won't always be like this: God will make everything new in the future, changing us and the sinful nature we battle with.

Providence in the mess

Providence, as we've seen, is God's ordering of his world. And this ordering means that our mess is no surprise to him, nor does it spoil his plans for us. Our bad decisions, made in sin or ignorance, do not stop the Lord's work in us and in his world. We can trust that none of it is outside his providence. He is bringing all things to completion.[3]

My husband's favourite Puritan, Thomas Watson, describes the providence of God wonderfully in a section of his book, *A Body of Practical Divinity*:

> The providence of God is 'the queen and governess of the world': it is the eye that sees, and the hand that turns all the wheels in the universe. God is not like an artificer that builds a house, and then leaves it, but like a pilot He steers the ship of the whole creation . . . Suppose you were in a smith's shop, and should see there several sorts of tools, some crooked, some bowed, others hooked, would you condemn all these things, because they do not look handsome? The smith makes use of them all for doing his work. Thus it is with the providences of God; they seem to us to be very crooked and strange, yet they all carry on God's work.[4]

Paul actually boasted about his weakness because he knew that his security was not in himself and his own performance, but in Christ and his completed work on the cross. Thomas Watson knew that the crooked things, like personal difficulties or even our own sin, are used by the Lord in ways which we could never dream or imagine.

We don't know what weakness it was that Paul spoke about in 2 Corinthians: a physical disability, a difficult relationship or a temptation to sin. It can be very appealing to conceal our weaknesses, from ourselves and from others. Others might think less of us if they saw the state of the inside of our cooker, or that our cakes were shop-bought, or that we didn't have a quiet time this morning, not even a short one. But, in God's providence, they might just find us more approachable or be able to share their own weaknesses with us. Our lack of perfection can be used by God to reach others who are struggling. And he uses it to keep us humble: I can never think myself righteous when I remember the argument with my son about his homework and my lack of grace towards a forgetful daughter. This is not to excuse my sin, but to see that, even in my sin, God is working in me.

You wouldn't think it from the state of my house, but I actually have a bit of a perfectionist streak. In my imagination, I can see how brilliantly something could be done, and then it's very hard for me to half-do it or do it without the right pen or less than perfectly. I often feel I'd rather just skip it altogether than make a mess of it, or I leave it for 'later' – an imaginary time that never seems to arrive. God's providence reminds me that even doing a bit of something is worthwhile. So, it is truly better to read my Bible a little rather than not at all, even if I take ten years to do the Bible-in-a-year project I had planned. It's better to do a smattering of housework badly rather than none at all. If something's worth doing, it's worth doing badly – we don't know what God, in his providence, will achieve with our mess for his great purposes.

As the writer to the Hebrews reminds us, we can find mercy and grace to help, and God understands our weaknesses:

Since then we have a great high priest who has passed through the heavens, Jesus, the Son of God, let us hold fast our confession. For we do not have a high priest who is unable to sympathize with our weaknesses, but one who in every respect has been tempted as we are, yet without sin. Let us then with confidence draw near to the throne of grace, that we may receive mercy and find grace to help in time of need. (Hebrews 4:14–16)

Jesus knows all about us and our messy lives which reflect our messy hearts. And yet, he wants us to be holy, as he is holy, and he calls us to be perfect (1 Peter 1:16; Matthew 5:48). He also sympathizes with our struggles to become holy and wants us to access his mercy and grace when we fail. I need to remind myself of that regularly and not hold on to my guilt nor allow it to stop me growing like him, however haphazardly. I need to remember his grace and providence in the mess. It is Christ who changes me, and he wants me to be, in the right sense of the term, a perfect mess.

2. Messy house

High Victorian ceilings and spacious Victorian rooms? We got 'em. Rattling single-glazed sash windows which let Arctic gales rip through the house? That's us. And freezing temperatures due to lack of funds for heating large and draughty rooms with lofty ceilings? Welcome to our vicarage: absolutely perfect for a real Christmas tree. The chill means that the needles don't drop too readily over the Christmas season, and the room height means we can choose a tall and elegant tree. The needles always fall off in great handfuls when the tree is being removed though. Of course. They scatter themselves artistically all over the living room floor and then spread evenly along the hallway, right out into the drive, where the tree then stays for a few weeks or months, until we can be organized enough to take it to the tip. Or whatever it is that happens to the tree – I normally forget its destiny on an annual basis.

One of the lovely things about having a real tree is how it leaves little mementos of Christmas which last throughout the year. Or it does if your housekeeping pattern is similar to mine. Of course, once the tree makes its way out of the front door, the hoover is drafted in to cut through the carpet of needles. With parishioners coming into the house on a regular basis, I can't get away with totally avoiding all chores at all times. But some of the pointy little green leaves stick themselves into the carpet, and others make their way under the furniture or into the gap between carpet and skirting board. And there they lie for most of the subsequent months, taking me back to Christmas, sparkly lights and the wonder of the incarnation, but also reminding me that I would almost certainly fail every housekeeping exam going, and should probably try vacuuming with the weird pointy attachment thing at some stage.

Obviously, the state of your home (and number of pine needles still embedded in the carpet in July) will vary depending on your tolerance of mess, the other things on your to-do list and the help you have available. You'll have worked out by now that my mess tolerance is really rather high. There always seems to be something more interesting to do than wiping down the top of the fridge. Also more interesting than hoovering, dusting, mopping or doing the washing-up or the laundry. But since my current full-time job is to take care of the house and family, I don't really have any good excuses for avoiding these things. My children are still, alas, too young to be of much help, though some promising progress is being made with laundry fetching and the recycling. My husband helps out a fair bit, specializing in bins and chopping wood for the fire, and so do our ministry trainee lodgers, who muck in with the all-too-frequent dishwasher loads and washing-up, but the organizing and planning and general management of the house is still my baby.

So how can I get the right balance in a world of perfect homes, where the show home with the latest style of wallpaper is the template we're told to aspire to? And does God have a view on the state of my skirting boards? If I live in my house, it will get messy regularly – dishes will need to be washed, baths will need to be scoured. If I'm able to pay someone else to clean, I will still bear some responsibility for what is cleaned and whether this person can actually find the things that need dusting beneath all the clutter. How should I think about this mundane work which is never finished?

The man and woman created by God are given a job to do, right at the beginning of the Bible:

So God created man in his own image,
   in the image of God he created him;
   male and female he created them.

And God blessed them. And God said to them, 'Be fruitful and multiply and fill the earth and subdue it and have dominion over the fish of the sea and over the birds of the heavens and over every living thing that moves on the earth.'
(Genesis 1:27–28)

Our home is part of the earth that God has given us to subdue. And it's hard work subduing things, especially after Adam and Eve ate the fruit and the ground became cursed (Genesis 3:17). So, God does have a view on my skirting boards: his command to me is to subdue them. And I'm not sure I'm tackling this as well as I should. If at all, to be honest. So, where do I go when faced with piles of laundry, tea to be made and an urgent need for space to be cleared on the living room carpet?

The mess just grows and grows. Or shrinks and grows again. And once again I am guilty and stressed and my relationships are suffering. I need to know what my house is for and see how God's grace and providence can help me when my house is defeating me.

What is a house for?

Our vicarage is a strange sort of house because it's a place of work as well as a place for rest. Other homes are increasingly doubling up as offices, so working from home is not all that unusual any more. We generally manage to confine most vicaring work to my husband's study, but visitors often spill into other parts of the house too. And so do the vicar and other church staff when temperatures plummet. You see, the vicar's study is the coldest room (temperatures well below the legal working minimum are pretty standard in winter). In fact, I wonder if the house was built that way to encourage clergy to do lots of visiting? Whatever the work done in a home, though, every home that contains a Christian is a place for ministry, whether official or

unofficial. So, it's good to think about what God wants me to do with the space I inhabit.

The place we live in always serves two purposes, even if it's not a workplace: it is a space for rest and a space for relationships. In the Bible, 'house' is a word used to refer to families themselves (Psalm 135:19) and not just the space in which they live and find shelter. So the house of God is the temple, but it is also his people. Wherever his people are, that is God's house. This means that the scruffy student flat is God's house just as much as the bishop's palace or the ancient church building.

Tips from the vicarage: House

1. **Clearing up:** A vital part of housekeeping is ensuring the safety of visitors. This starts with the avoidance of serious injury on entry to the home. My aim is to keep the hallway clear enough so that visitors do not break bones on entering, falling over shoes, swimming bags or boxes of Sunday school crafts. This is harder to achieve than you might think. But it's worth persevering.

2. **Cleaning:** Everyone has a different level of clean that they find they can live with. It's fine to assume that anyone visiting has, at most, the same level as you do. They will notice far less than you think or be too polite to comment anyway. In the interests of harmony, it may be necessary to adjust cleaning frequency to suit household members, however. And to ensure that no major epidemics break out.

3. **Laundry:** It is a well-known fact that, left unattended, laundry can grow to occupy space which may be better used for eating, sitting or sleeping. A laundry mountain the size of Ben Nevis (scalable in a day) is acceptable. Once Everest proportions are reached, you should probably draft in some help. You may be surprised how many items of clothing can be worn unironed while still avoiding a look of complete dishevelment. Patting and folding can be surprisingly effective. Encourage an informal look for any vicars in your family. Clerical shirts, especially 100% cotton ones: OUT, polo shirts: IN.

4. **Garden:** An overgrown garden is best ignored. Going by the weather over the last few summers, there are only a couple of weeks in the year that you can spend in it anyway. As long as grass is occasionally mowed, most other things will die back in winter. The drafting of children into gardening work, involving payment per trug of weeds, is recommended. As long as you are happy to be flexible about the definition of weeds.

> 5. **Winter survival:** Vicarages are cold. Big houses and small
> stipends are not a warm match. And with the increasing costs of
> gas and electricity, even smaller, less draughty houses are being
> kept cooler. I recommend layering: scarves, two pairs of socks
> with furry lined boots, hot-water bottles and positioning
> yourself wherever the cat has curled up. The vicarage feline
> recommends the sofa or a fleece blanket on a bed. Perfect.

A house is for rest

So if my house is God's house, because God's people live there, what
sort of rest will be found there? Will it be like stepping into a five-star
hotel, with staff available to meet my every need, fluffy towels in the
bathroom, and sauna and gym available round the clock? Though this
may be something I'd love to have, this isn't the rest that God offers.

God's rest is a theme woven throughout the Bible, beginning with
the rest God took on the seventh day (Genesis 2:2) and leading us
to the rest found when everything is brought to completion in Christ
(Revelation 14:13). Jesus is the one who offers that rest: 'Come to me,
all who labour and are heavy laden, and I will give you rest. Take my
yoke upon you, and learn from me, for I am gentle and lowly in heart,
and you will find rest for your souls' (Matthew 11:28–29).

So, a house where we can rest is one where we are able to come
to Jesus. It's a house where we can lay down our burdens. It does not
need to be a show home. If I can find space to put the shopping down
and find a corner to sit and read my Bible, I can rest. It does not need
to have super shiny windows, although if they are so submerged
in smeary fingermarks that I can't see out of them and the sunlight
can't penetrate them, I won't be able to read that Bible. If I can
come home and lay down the cares of the day, the stress of a work
deadline or worries about a client, and find rest in God, then my
house is OK.

Susanna Wesley was the mother of the founders of Methodism,
John and Charles. A godly woman with a large family, her house was
so busy at times that the only 'space' she could find was under her

apron in the middle of a busy kitchen. Under an apron in a noisy place is not ideal, but it was better than nothing – she was able to rest in God in a space that was less than perfect. I remember being surprised the first time I prayed with a friend while we kept our eyes open. We were supervising her small children playing in a park – it was before my own children were born. It wasn't what I was used to at all, and we were sometimes interrupted by a tumble from a swing or distracted by people passing by. But we prayed. We found our rest in God. This was far better than not praying at all because we were looking for some sort of ideal and unattainable situation of silence and calm.

A house is for relationships

My house is where I experience my closest relationships, living with family but also inviting in the people I am, or want to be, close to. So, when I tidy the living room, my primary motivation is so that those in the house can rest and relate to one another. We *can* sit together surrounded by piles of paper, dirty mugs, biscuit crumbs and a collection of damp coats. Yes, it's physically possible, but actually, we find our relating is better, and our resting is better, if we clear ourselves some more space and get away from the distractions.

So, I love to have a tidy living room and a clear kitchen table. But on all those days when I've not had time or energy to bring order to the chaos, I can't turn away the person at the door who needs a cuppa and a chat. I need to look to God and seek his grace, so that this opportunity for ministry is used for his glory. I need to learn how to find rest in the mess, so that relationships can grow.

If the messy state of my house or my need to keep it looking pristine stops me from following Christ and serving others, I need to fix it, either by tidying up or by chilling out when things aren't perfect. We're not always (actually more like hardly ever) prepared for callers who turn up unexpectedly. We've had people needing a chat appearing early on a Saturday morning when we're still in pyjamas and the remnants of a Friday-night takeaway are still strewn all over the kitchen table. It's no good turning someone away when I can make them a cuppa, throw on some clothes and chat as I gather up the containers of chicken tikka and pour a quick bowl of Crunchy Nut cornflakes. I need to clear up my attitude and expectations about the house. I need to think biblically about my home. Am I bothered so much by what others will think of it that I don't want them to come round until everything is perfect? Or is the state of the house such that I feel permanently stressed? Somewhere in the space between totally cluttered squalor and neat-freak shininess, we need to find a place of godly contentment.

Grace in the messy house

How can God's grace help me, when the space I live in is carpeted with life's detritus and I can't begin to bring order to bear? We've already seen that God has called the people he created to subdue the earth, so if I'm living in a mess which prevents rest in God and damages relationships, I have fallen short of his standards: I have sinned.

Somewhere in the space between totally cluttered squalor and neat-freak shininess, we need to find a place of godly contentment.

And when we have sinned, we know what to do: 'If we confess our sins, he is faithful and just to forgive us our sins and to cleanse us from all unrighteousness' (1 John 1:9).

As I seek his grace, God is willing and able to forgive me for my sloth or failure of priorities. But I need to be sure that my standard of messlessness is God's standard, one which enables rest and relationships. If I strive to meet a standard set by the world, by other people or by magazines, by TV programmes or an inner voice of perfectionism, I am likely to fail. I am also likely to spend time on housework that might be better spent with people or with God. If my house takes up all my energy and my concern, it could be that it has become my idol. If it has, then I need to recognize that and repent of it.

The standards of grace

In the course of our married life, my husband and I have lived in eight homes in five cities and one town spread across three countries. Our current home is the house that we've lived in the longest since we were married in 1995. This means that I have developed a domestic routine which includes the cleaning of curtain rails and ovens only when I move house. But now we've been here in the vicarage for four years, this is beginning to seem a little slovenly, even for me. The house is beginning to show signs of being unsubdued. In short, nearly four years of clutter have been preventing rest and healthy relationships.

So, we have taken things in hand and are beginning to tackle the house, room by room. The vicarage still doesn't look like a show home or anything that would appear in a magazine, but the piles of paper on a table in the living room have been sorted out, and a clear space on the living room carpet now appears more regularly than once in a blue moon.

As I consider God's grace, I can see that his offer of undeserved mercy means that I can press on with clearing up, without being weighed down by guilt. God's concern is that people are brought into relationship with him and able to enjoy his perfect rest. I need to apply that priority to my house and the standards I impose on it. I need to keep asking myself: how can I help people to rest here?

It's so easy to be sucked into the scenario sold to us by *How Clean Is Your House?* and similar programmes, which tell us that, if our houses are properly clean, then all other aspects of our lives will somehow be sorted too. But the gospel's message isn't that a clean house brings a clean heart. Only Jesus can bring a clean heart. He came to clean up our lives and bring people into relationship with him, so that we are able to enjoy his perfect rest. And I want people to meet the one true God in my house, not worship me as a domestic goddess.

'For God, who said, "Let light shine out of darkness", has shone in our hearts to give the light of the knowledge of the glory of God in the face of Jesus Christ' (2 Corinthians 4:6). God shines his light into our hearts to give us knowledge of God's glory. That is our priority. His rest, our relationship with him.

Grace with others

By the same token, I need God's grace when I visit someone else's house too. I have many friends who are a great deal tidier than me, but also a few who seem similarly submerged or even drowning in clutter. The temptation I face in someone else's house is to feel smug as I compare myself and find myself messier (Well done me, I'm not stressed by a bit of clutter!) or, on very rare occasions, tidier (Well done me, I'm a fantastic housekeeper!). Or it may be, if you have a less confident personality, that the comparison is more negative: 'My house will never be this spotless', or 'Why can't I relax when there's a bit of clutter around?'

This is where I need to resist the temptation to compare myself to someone else. By doing so, I am making other people (and their housekeeping skills or lack of them) the standard by which I judge myself. In fact, I am worshipping them. I am not looking to God's standard and considering whether my house is a place for rest and relationship. Instead, I am wondering whether I am better or worse than someone else, using a standard that I have created. And so, I need to seek God's grace and forgiveness for my sin of pride and the idolatrous heart that looks at the state of a kitchen and draws a false spiritual conclusion about my own or someone else's standing before the Lord.

Pride in my heart might also prevent me from accepting help when it is offered: 'No, no, I can cope . . .' How many of us have said that to a kind friend or relative? In the month or so just after my husband had started at theological college, while I was ill, a few folk from our campus community came round and helped us out, with meals, childcare and laundry. I didn't mind my mum coming to help – she knew and accepted me anyway. But having someone I barely knew sorting me out made me feel inadequate.

Of course, the truth is that I *was* inadequate, for the task of housekeeping while ill and pregnant, with a toddler in the house. And actually, that was fine. I wasn't any less a Christian or any less a mother and wife because I needed help. I needed to put away the façade of omnicompetence I was trying to project and accept whatever was on offer. Accepting the grace of others can be as hard as accepting God's grace, because our sinful hearts yet again want to earn what is freely offered.

If I have funds which enable me to pay someone else to clean my bathrooms regularly or nuke the cemented carbon deposits from the oven, then it is not a failure or an admission of weakness to do so. I need to see the money I can use for this as God's grace to enable me

to stay calm or offer more hospitality or spend time with my children or prevent the whole family coming down with botulism. If family or friends will help out for free, we need to remember God's grace to us and accept that help. Even if Auntie who's helping me is a little patronizing about my vast ironing pile, she's still doing the ironing, and that's better than being proud with a mountain of unironed mess that weighs me down.

And if I have received God's grace in my house, I am also called to help others out in their homes, if my own mess allows. And to do this graciously, for God's glory. I find that it's always so much easier to do someone else's ironing than my own, for reasons that are unfathomable. So do feel free to come over and start sorting mine out! It's quite astonishing how much has mounted up during the book-writing process. (Could you manage next week?)

In his first letter, Peter advises his readers how to go about serving one another:

> As each has received a gift, use it to serve one another, as good stewards
> of God's varied grace: whoever speaks, as one who speaks oracles of
> God; whoever serves, as one who serves by the strength that God
> supplies – in order that in everything God may be glorified through Jesus
> Christ. To him belong glory and dominion for ever and ever. Amen.
> (1 Peter 4:10–11)

Christians are called to steward God's grace in all its forms. That includes the grace of helping one another in the home and the grace of accepting the service of others. God will be glorified in our houses if we can learn to serve one another by the strength that God supplies, including helping one another to find rest.

Providence in the messy house

God is sovereign over the state of my house. He has put me in this house for his purposes at this point in my life. The story I told at the beginning of this book shows how, through his providence, my messy house at college enabled one friend to find me more approachable. If the space I live in is difficult to inhabit, because of sin or simply because of circumstances, looking for signs of God's providence will always encourage me.

Moving house and community every two or three years before we came to live in our current vicarage was not the ideal way to spend our first fourteen years of married life. But, in God's providence, our experience of living in so many different places has enabled us to relate better to the many immigrants in our community and to those forced to move on regularly because of poor accommodation or difficult circumstances. We've been blessed to see the outworking of God's providence in this aspect of our lives but, even when we are struggling to see this, remembering it will help us persevere when the house is in a state or difficult to live in. As Thomas Watson reminds us:

> The providences of God are sometimes dark, and our eyes dim, and we can hardly tell what to make of them; but when we cannot unriddle providence, let us believe that it will work together for the good of the elect. Rom 8:28. The wheels in a clock seem to move contrary one to the other – but they help forward the motion of the clock. Just so, the providences of God seem to be cross wheels; but for all that, they shall carry on the good of the elect.[1]

I love my big old house, with its whistling chimneys and sub-zero-temperature downstairs loo. There's plenty of space to spread out in and to welcome others into. But when my husband was first ordained, we lived in a tiny house without even enough space for our furniture (which we had to leave in storage) or even our winter clothes (which got a bit tricky come November). When I first looked at the house, before my husband had accepted the job, the duct tape holding one kitchen drawer together fell off and the drawer collapsed. Nomadic tenants had lived in the house for a couple of years, and there had been almost no maintenance for many more. I cried.

My husband still accepted that curacy in Wolverhampton on the basis that there's far more to a curacy than the house. And we were very happy there indeed, both in the small house with the collapsing kitchen and in a rather larger and far more suitable one which was made available about eight months later, the diocese having decided that the original house was indeed too small and rickety for our family.

In God's providence, the first house was an ideal place to begin our work with the small youth group – its large kitchen allowed us to host happy evenings and open up the Bible with them. Looking back, we can see that God wanted us to be there first. We made good friends with some of the neighbours, who we continued to see even after we'd moved. It was in a quiet area, so we were able to settle down in the town before we moved more into the thick of it – our new house was closer to the busy hub of the parish. Yes, it was a house we could be thankful for. We found God's rest there and built new relationships with neighbours and church members, and strengthened our relationships within our family. So, the house with the decrepit drawers worked together for our good, even though that was hard to anticipate at first viewing.

Wherever I'm living, God's Word reminds me, as it did Thomas Watson, that he will work for the good of his people: 'And we know that for those who love God all things work together for good, for those who are called according to his purpose' (Romans 8:28).

The roof over my head will bring possibilities for ministry and growth in my faith that are often impossible to anticipate in advance. I can thank God for my messy house, because in it I can find his rest and nurture my relationships with him and with others. The unchanging God is the same, and his providences are always for my good.

3. Messy family

'Let me introduce you to the person most likely to murder you . . .'

This was the arresting opening line we were expecting in the first marriage preparation session with our minister. In the church where my husband and I celebrated our wedding, all engaged couples attended marriage preparation sessions with various church members before the big day. The final meetings were with the vicar himself. We were part of a busy congregation where there were quite a few weddings every year, and news got round, so we thought we knew what to expect when we tipped up at the vicarage. There was a rumour that our minister would shock us at the beginning of our meeting with the startling statement about marital homicide quoted above.

We were rather disappointed that he didn't actually say that – in fact he denied it being his standard opener at all. But he did point out that in marriage we would both be living intimately with another sinner. And that this would be a great source of frustration as well as a major way for God to change and sanctify each of us, making us holy and more like Jesus. This was a helpful and realistic perspective as we began married life and started a new family together.

Family is one of God's primary ways of making us more like Christ. Here we live intimately with other sinners. Those who know us best always know our weaknesses. They know which buttons to press to rile us. And we know their fallenness too and how we can bring them down with just a few words. Family members know our iniquities better than anyone else. We can perhaps hide a few things from them, the secret parts of our lives that only the Lord knows about, but generally our family know the real people underneath the fancy dressing we employ with those who know us less well.

To paraphrase Tolstoy: tidy families are all alike; every messy family is messy in its own way. And the sinfulness of human beings means that every family is a messy family. In its own way. Messy families have been with us since the expulsion from Eden: Adam and Eve's family mess included a son who murdered his brother. I remember when I was quite young, how a family crisis stretched us all. My parents then shared with me a few stories about other families we knew, all outwardly thriving and happy. But, truthfully, each of these families had struggles and difficulties that were different from ours, but still comparable in scale. A messy family is actually pretty normal.

What is family?

In *The Archer and the Arrow*, Phillip Jensen describes the aim of his ministry as 'to preach the gospel by prayerfully expounding [carefully explaining and applying] the Bible to the people God has given me to love'.[1]

His description of a church as 'the people God has given me to love' can apply equally to the family. Family can be defined in many ways, but, for the purposes of this chapter, I want to define family as 'our nearest and dearest' or 'the people God has given me to love'. So, that includes our relations, especially those we live or have lived with. But it also includes lodgers, flatmates and friends, who often take on the role of family members, sometimes temporarily. We certainly don't choose to be part of the family we came from – they are given to us by God. Nor do we choose the children given to us. And although, in our Western culture, we normally choose a husband or wife, a spouse is also given to us by God. And the people who end up being lodgers, flatmates and friends are also within God's sovereignty.

Another way of looking at family might be to think of them as 'the people you can fart in front of' (as a friend suggested to me the other day, although you may well disagree). It's a reminder that the family is the network of relationships where we take less care to cover over our unpleasantness – whether it be merely thoughtless flatulence or something much more serious.

Extended family

Over the years, I've lived with close family and had a variety of house-mates and lodgers. I've been a lodger myself and stayed in a couple of company messes when I worked overseas. (A mess is a house rented by the firm for long- and short-term stays.) Over that time, a colleague and I developed a name for the extra depth of relationship you found with your workmates when you lived with them. We called it 'the knee factor'. You relate very differently to senior management once you've seen them in their shorts or seen their laundry drying on the line. In a brief couple of months overseas, living and working together, colleagues would become your family.

We've had a few extra members in our family since we've lived in the vicarage, as we've hosted ministry trainees, and a couple of others, in the attic. They've seen us in the mornings when we're grumpy and uncaffeinated. They've heard us shouting at the children or bickering with each other. They've annoyed us by some minor habit that really begins to grate after the nineteenth occurrence. They've prayed, laughed and cried with us in the daily strains of family and ministry life. They've been woken at 6am by the gentleman of the road who regularly camps in our front garden. They've known both our best efforts and our worst messes and are still speaking to us. They've sometimes (poor them) encountered our noxious bodily odours. That makes them family – and a part of the mess.

Grace in the family

I may already have mentioned that in family life I frequently need to seek God's grace for forgiveness. This is where I see my selfishness most, my desire to serve myself and not others. So many things I fail to do, so many other occasions when I take the easy route for my own comfort, rather than following Christ's example of humility and service. My personal speciality is faffing about, wasting time – on the internet or in some other more creative way – and then being stressed and flappy as a deadline approaches, usually one for leaving the house or feeding children before leaving the house. My children are consequently growing up learning to eat extremely fast. But I need to learn habits of grace when I feel like I'm losing control.

In Paul Tripp's helpful book on the basics of counselling, *Instruments in the Redeemer's Hands*, he clarifies personal responsibility very clearly. There are areas of life and relationships that are my responsibility, where I need to obey God faithfully. So, my procrastination and flapping are my responsibility, areas of life which I need to change. Outside of that is the area of my concern: things that I need to entrust to God. So, the response of my family to my sin, or to my godliness, is not something I can personally change.

As I think about family relationships, I need to think about what depends on me and let the Lord deal with the things that don't. I need to reflect on the verse: 'If possible, so far as it depends on you, live peaceably with all' (Romans 12:18).

If I know that God's grace has paid for my sins, I am able to remember that I can be forgiven for the bitterness I feel towards the relative who made me feel small at the family gathering. More than that, if I can remember God's grace before bitterness takes hold, I will know his peace rather than the pain of resentment. Grace leads me to heaven, so I can learn to be gracious in my reply to the second cousin who sent that smug Christmas letter detailing the stupendous achievements of her offspring and grandchildren, while our family was struggling through ill health and poor GCSE grades. Grace leads me to heaven, and that is the place I need to keep fixed in my head as

I negotiate those family relationships with all their broken history and kaleidoscope of joyful and painful memories.

Family is where we usually sin most often, and so family relationships are the relationships where we will need to exercise grace most often too. Seeking daily forgiveness, in my experience, is an essential part of family life. That's why we pray a confession in the vicarage every teatime. We find it very helpful to have daily space to mend relationships and offer grace to one another. And it's no wonder there's an Anglican prayer for grace in families, which is often used in services:

> Give grace to us, our families and friends, and to all our neighbours, that we may serve Christ in one another, and love as he loves us.[2]

Family is where I find the biggest challenge to, and the greatest need for, the regular exercise of grace. So, I need to pray for that grace and desire it for myself. I need to recognize that seeking rest in my relationship with God will help me to grow in grace, so that my family relationships will grow more restful too.

Family mess

I quite enjoy creating crafty things, but never stick with one sort of craft for very long. Adding to vicarage clutter therefore are collections of abandoned projects stuffed into boxes and cupboards. One such collection is composed of the remnants of a kit I put together to make friendship bracelets on a Christian summer holiday for young people

Family is where we usually sin most often, and so family relationships are the area where we will need to exercise grace most often too.

a few years ago. The main component is brightly coloured cotton yarn. But if I'm ever to try the activity again, I fear I may have a long session of untangling ahead of me. The following equation applies here:

Teenagers + multiple yarns kept close together
+ limited time + limited patience
= a frustrating stringy morass of yarn spaghetti

Family relationships likewise contain multiple threads of life, often in close proximity with many limits on time and patience, and so we end up facing a frustrating messy tangle of family life.

The pages of Scripture are filled with stories of messy families. The curse on Eve following the meeting with the serpent and the eating of the fruit of the tree of the knowledge of good and evil in Genesis 3 shows us how it all began:

To the woman he said,

'I will surely multiply your pain in childbearing;
    in pain you shall bring forth children.
Your desire shall be for your husband,
    and he shall rule over you.'
(Genesis 3:16)

So, pain in parenting and frustration in marriage are the results of the fall. They have been with us ever since the beginning of humanity. And therefore, to our regret, the daily vicarage routine includes spouses bickering about the storage of plastic tubs, children who sulk for a couple of hours over a minor dispute, and multiple rows about apple cores, plum stones and sweetie wrappers strewn about the house.

If we move to the New Testament and look at the great cloud of witnesses of Hebrews 11 who are commended for their faith, we see the names of many people with seriously dysfunctional families. We don't have full details of their family lives in the Bible snapshots, but we can see enough to recognize the sin which corrupts their family relationships. And ours. Noah was a drunk who cursed the son who caught him naked. Abraham's son, Isaac, tricked his brother into selling his birthright for a bowl of stew and deceived his father into blessing him. David's family history included estrangement, adultery, murder and seriously rebellious children, one of whom killed a brother and then tried to usurp his father and even went into battle against him. Jephthah made a hasty vow and ended up offering his only daughter as a sacrifice to fulfil it.

Joseph's brothers tried to kill him and then sold him into slavery. His brothers' families were also pretty messy: with twelve brothers, the opportunities for fallings out and relational catastrophes are obviously significant. Multiple close relationships can go wrong in many ways. Yet, through all these families, God was working out his salvation purposes. As Joseph, despite all his sufferings and mistreatment, says, 'As for you, you meant evil against me, but God meant it for good, to bring it about that many people should be kept alive, as they are today' (Genesis 50:20).

All the women in the genealogy of Christ found in Matthew 1 had messy families: Tamar's sons were a result of her pretending to be a prostitute with her father-in-law; Rahab was in fact a prostitute; Ruth's husband died and she ended up caring for an embittered mother-in-law; Bathsheba's husband was killed by her lover, and Mary became pregnant before her marriage and, because of appearances, was nearly dumped by her fiancé.

If I consider these relationally catastrophic Bible families, I am encouraged by remembering that God achieves everything he sets out to achieve through his people, despite their sinful behaviour and broken relationships. I can see his providence working through messy families. It reminds me that he will work out his purposes through my messy family, no matter what that mess might be.

Family change

If my physical bricks-and-mortar house is my space for rest and relationships, then my family, especially my household, provide the relationships where that rest is lived out. And yet, it often seems that with family can be the least restful place in the world to be. On Saturdays, our family like to eat tea in front of the telly. Most times, my hardworking husband uses this opportunity to fall asleep. While the rest of us are enjoying an episode of our favourite box set, he will gently begin to snore on the sofa. So, occasionally, he's able to rest with the family, and I think this brief window may be his peak rest time. But it often seems that most parenting hours are spent refereeing disputes between warring children, clearing up scattered clothing and finding the lost piece of the game we were about to try and play to stop the argument.

Families make a mess, and, the more of you living together, the bigger that mess. In fact, I'm pretty sure that mess grows exponentially with the number of people added to the mix. And family mess is not just about the laundry and bits of Lego; it's also about the complexity of relationships lived out with people who see you in sharp focus.

One of the ways God works in us is by bringing change into our lives. Very often I find that, if I pray to grow, for example, more patient, then God will put me in situations where I will have to exercise patience. This difficult situation enables me to grow in faith and Christlikeness.

So a change in the make-up of the household: a new lodger in the vicarage, for example, is an opportunity for us all to grow in godliness as we adapt to the change this brings. And because children change enormously as they grow up, their presence in a house ensures that the adults are brought to their knees, seeking God's help, at extremely regular intervals. The church where I was married had a vision statement which concluded: 'We believe that God means us to grow, individually and as a church; that growth is change; and that change may be painful. We accept the pain of change gladly for the sake of bringing the gospel to our contemporaries.'[3]

A vision for a church can apply equally well to a family. If we want the gospel brought into the lives of everyone God has given us to love, then that will mean painful change as we learn to relate to them in Christlike ways. I must ask myself: how much am I prepared to change for the sake of bringing the gospel to my family?

When I got married, I had to change my habit of leaving all the drawers in my chest of drawers open. My new husband liked a tidier bedroom than I was used to keeping, so I changed. Mostly. I hate damp bathmats left on the floor. So he learnt to pick the bathmat up. And to leave the loo seat down. Those were small adjustments to our tidiness habits, though I'm still (eighteen years of marriage later) working on some of them. Habits of speech or thinking are far more difficult to address. Change for the sake of my family may need more than an alteration in a drawer-closing routine.

Tim Chester addresses how we might accomplish this in his excellent book *You Can Change*. He approaches change with four great truths about God:

1. God is great – so we don't have to be in control
2. God is glorious – so we don't have to fear others
3. God is good – so we don't have to look elsewhere
4. God is gracious – so we don't have to prove ourselves

Chester says, 'There's much more to be said about God than is covered by these four truths, but they offer a powerful diagnostic tool for addressing most of the sins and emotions with which we struggle.'[4]

I can accept that my family will always be messy this side of glory, but I still need to change so that I can bring the gospel to them and love these people given to me by God. There are many ways in which God, by his Spirit, will help me to do that, and working through *You Can Change* offers a helpful way to address specific areas. Acceptance that family is messy is in no way an acceptance of my own sin or a recognition that I do not need to change. God wants to change me. Yes, it is likely to be painful and messy. But it is always worth it. Think how lovely it is to have a dry bathmat. And a chest with all its drawers closed.

Providence in the family

Our family lives in a pretty deprived area: it's about 300th from bottom on a register of deprivation of over 12,000 parishes in England and Wales. But both my husband and I grew up in middle-class families and comfortable middle-class areas. In God's providence, the security and stability of our backgrounds have enabled us to persevere in serving in places where many families lack both. More trivially, we both come from families who love to eat spicy food. My parents conducted their courtship over curry as students in London in the 1960s, when most of England still ate potatoes with everything. This is a brilliant background in a place where so many people add chilli to their meals and our local pub speciality is barbecued tandoori chicken.

Others have had far more painful experiences of the providence of God through their families. Edinburgh pastor Mez McConnell's childhood was full of pain, but his brokenness ultimately led him to Christ. The believing mother of one of our friends from the parish recently died from cancer. Losing his mum was one of the factors that led our friend to turn from his addiction to heroin and embrace the Christian faith.

God's providence in our family may be painful in the extreme, but Thomas Boston reminds us that Christians 'have ground for the greatest encouragement and comfort in the middle of all the events of providence, seeing they are managed by their covenant God and gracious friend, who will never neglect or overlook his dear people, and whatever concerns them. For he hath said, "I will never leave thee, nor forsake thee," Heb. [13:]5.'[5]

Just as my sin affects my children as they grow up, so my personality and character and general habits of sin have been partly shaped by the sins of previous generations. I tend to sin more like my own parents and grandparents than like other people's parents and grandparents. As the deadline for this book approaches, for example, I try to resist the temptation to procrastinate because I can't craft a perfect sentence. Thanks Mum! Thanks Dad! I know just where that faffing-about-followed-by-late-nights-trying-to-get-it-just-right habit comes from.

In the book of Exodus, Moses collects the tablets carved with the Ten Commandments on two occasions (see Exodus 32:1–24 for the context, which includes Israel's idolatry and the breaking of the first set of tablets). While he is at the top of Mount Sinai with the tablets on the second occasion, God speaks:

The LORD passed before him and proclaimed, 'The LORD, the LORD, a God merciful and gracious, slow to anger, and abounding in steadfast love and faithfulness, keeping steadfast love for thousands, forgiving iniquity and transgression and sin, but who will by no means clear the guilty, visiting the iniquity of the fathers on the children and the children's children, to the third and the fourth generation.'
(Exodus 34:6–7)

A tendency to procrastinate is not the only sin-method inherited or learnt as we grow up. When I think of my upbringing, I am so grateful for the many good things, but I'm also able to see patterns of sin that I learnt too. Like father, like daughter. Like mother, like son. Like granny, like grandson. And some of those messy sin patterns are particularly evident when I relate, as an adult, to the people who knew me when I was growing up.

It's so easy to revert to bad old habits of behaviour, letting our childhood selves take over from the grown-ups we've become. The childhood self that stays with parents, yet fails to help with the washing-up because we didn't help when we were eight. The childhood self that reacts to parental pressure or expectations with all the emotional incontinence of a fifteen-year-old, despite our now being thirty-seven with a serious career. How do we rest in God's grace when that great-aunt who's always undermined us is around for Christmas? And is our family life messier than it should be because we're still behaving like children?

As the adult child of an adult, I need to recognize when the mess I am making in my family relationships is old mess. There's mess I need to leave behind. There's other mess I need to learn to live with. And maybe some mess I need to tidy up. I need to let my family be glad, so far as it depends on me.

The father of the righteous will greatly rejoice;
    he who fathers a wise son will be glad in him.
Let your father and mother be glad;
    let her who bore you rejoice.
(Proverbs 23:24–25)

We all know that the closeness of family relationships means that families are the context in which most pain can be caused. A cutting word from an aunt usually bears far more weight than one from a neighbour. Perhaps the family are a source of embarrassment. My father's aunt caused him some blushes when he was a student in London in the 1950s. Travelling up an escalator on the Tube with a friend, he exclaimed, 'Oh, it's my aunt!' Looking round for a woman with a family likeness to my father, his friend was puzzled until my dad pointed out some adverts on a wall. For corsets, starring my scantily clad great-aunt.

In God's providence, his ordering of our world, we also inherit other characteristics from our families: an irreverent sense of humour or a love of peach melba ice cream, a fondness for 1930s jazz or a capacity for tenacity in research, whether for a work project or in a choice of sofa. We learn to appreciate strong blue cheese because our flatmate shares theirs with us, or we watch our lodger and learn from their habits of organization. In all that we have passed on to us through family, God is bringing about his good purposes. He never neglects or overlooks his people.

Tips from the vicarage: Family visits, phones and laundry

1. **Visits:** Family visiting from afar are a great encouragement and tonic. We are thankful therefore that our vicarage has space to accommodate visiting relations and others. We do find, however, that a visit date, set in the diary several months ago, is bound to clash horribly with additional preaching engagements (not for me, thankfully), several funerals, a major pastoral crisis in the congregation and a vicarage child coming down with mumps or some other toxic and easily transmittable disease.

2. **Phones:** Special ringtones for cheering calls from family far away ensure perkiness even before speaking to that favourite auntie who's supplying her special recipe, or Grandad calling us

with a new joke. It can also be used to screen out grizzly Cousin Greta who always wants you to come and visit at Easter weekend or on some other impossible church-heavy occasion.

3. **Laundry:** In my experience, mothers and mothers-in-law are always very kind about washing and ironing things when they come to the vicarage. The over-full laundry baskets they encounter on every visit, however, are a result of incompetence rather than planning. Honest. I was truly thinking I'd have it all sorted before they arrived. But then, you know, er, it wasn't.

4. Messy kids

I was once on my way to a reading group when my two eldest children were very small. I think my daughter may have been about two and a half and her brother six months old or so. It was before their youngest brother had been born. The kids were going to be looked after in a crèche, while I spent some much-needed adult time discussing a Christian book with two other women, both students and wives of students at the same theological college as my husband. I had been looking forward to this adult time very much.

Before the meeting, I took a few minutes to deal with some email correspondence. The kids were playing quietly on the landing outside the bedroom, and my daughter asked if she could do some colouring, so I distractedly agreed. I emerged after about five minutes. There, to my horror, was my daughter with a bright red permanent marker pen in her hand and red marks on the carpet, the bookshelf, the wall, the bedroom door, her brother's striped dungarees and all over her brother's face. My son looked like he was suffering from a severe comedy case of the measles.

My neglect and distraction landed us with a lot of mess that day. I was late for my reading group; we had paintwork to clean, a defaced bookshelf to sort out, months of carpet washing ahead of us, dungarees

which ended up in the bin, but, most depressingly of all, I forgot to take a photograph of my little boy's face.

As every mother will tell you, children create mess at every turn, from nappies to toddler tantrums at the front of the church, from glitter sprayed over the carpet to screaming altercations about using the computer. As they grow up, the type of mess they create will change, confusing us just as we think we have the parenting thing sussed. We don't, but God's wisdom will help us to steer our way through the choppy waters of family life.

Children are a church

'Would you like a couple of steaks? Or how about four bags of oranges?'

Just the sort of question a family struggling to live on a tight budget at theological college likes to be asked. Some friends had sent an online order to Asda, and somehow the computer system had contrived to order every single item they'd ever had delivered in the past. There were crates and crates and crates of cereal, meat, vegetables, fruit and sundry other random items. As our friends started to point this out, they were told that the mistake was the supermarket's, so they could keep everything and wouldn't be charged a penny. It was an unexpected gift for their family – and for ours too, as the perishable items were shared out among the neighbours.

Children are a gift from God, as Solomon tells us in Psalm 127. They may not be just what we thought we'd ordered, nor everything we've ever ordered, and the way they turn out is often a surprise. And a good surprise at that:

> Behold, children are a heritage from the LORD,
>   the fruit of the womb a reward.
> (Psalm 127:3)

Solomon tells us that children are also arrows (in verse 4). Arrows can be directed. In his Bible commentary, Matthew Henry tells us, in his inimitable style, that the mark that these arrows are aimed at is God's glory and the service of our children's generation:

> Children of the youth are arrows in the hand, which, with prudence, may be directed aright to the mark, God's glory, and the service of their generation; but afterwards, when they are gone abroad in the world, they are arrows out of the hand; it is too late to bend them then . . . All earthly comforts are uncertain, but the Lord will assuredly comfort and bless those who serve him; and those who seek the conversion of sinners, will find that their spiritual children are their joy and crown in the day of Jesus Christ.[1]

As a parent, I can see that God has given me my children to love. Remember Phillip Jensen's description of a church family. These weren't the children I ordered! They are so different from what I expected. But God has given them to me, for my good as well as theirs, for his glory and the service of their generation. He may also (or instead) have given me godchildren, or other spiritual children, as Matthew Henry points out. But my aim as a parent is that my own children will be my spiritual children too, despite the mess this makes.

So my children are a mini church: a gathering of people we have been given to teach about God. And I have found that they behave in similar ways to an adult congregation. Apart from a love of quiche and coffee perhaps. They dislike change and would usually rather lead themselves. They grow best when taught the Bible and when they learn to follow the example of the Lord Jesus. New additions to the 'congregation' may be treated with suspicion at first, before acceptance comes. There are messy relationships with one another and with the pastor.

In the future, I pray that my kids will follow Christ for themselves, but, until they do that, my husband and I have to lead them. We are aiming arrows, so we need to have our own eyes on the mark. In that way, I can point the way for my kids until they are ready to be led by Jesus themselves.

Messy babies

Everyone knows that babies are messy, puking and pooing 24/7. No mother is fully dressed without a shoulder patch of white milk clots. Parents compete with tales of exploding nappies or projectile vomits in increasingly inappropriate situations. The tiredness, isolation and feelings of inadequacy among carers of a new baby can be overwhelming. You look a mess; you feel a mess, and, NB, this is *only the beginning* of parenting.

The big challenge for parents of small babies is to maintain godliness in spite of extreme physical exhaustion. Sometimes, you are so addled you forget all sorts of important things. One vicar's wife friend took her new baby to church in the pram. During post-service refreshments in the church hall, the sleeping baby was pushed into a quiet corner. Later, at home, my friend was enjoying a bit of peace and quiet when the ghastly realization dawned. Her offspring was still at church.

I only forgot my son very briefly, but it caused disproportionate disruption. I'd got him ready to go for his first outing with his sister and granny. We were heading out for a quick lunch and shop between feeds, and he was all ready and wrapped up in his padded suit and strapped into his car seat. My mother-in-law set off for the car, and I went to fix his sister in her seat, grabbing my handbag and shutting the front door. I was just preparing to start the car when my mother-in-law reminded me about the baby. Shut behind the front door. And my front door keys were inside too.

Thankfully, this happened when my husband was at theological college. So he (and his front door keys) were very close by, although engrossed in the middle of a lecture. Which I had to interrupt. So, my boy spent about ten minutes on his own in the locked house. Needless to say, my mortification lasted a good deal longer. No harm done though. I always think it's a great blessing that children remember very few specific incidents from their early years. So, I can reassure myself by remembering that a general impression of safety and care will always outweigh occasional lapses of parenting competence.

I was sustained through the baby phase of my children's lives by frequent naps and a very relaxed attitude to housework. That was when I met my friend who found me less-than-intimidating because of the state of my home. Useful advice: your children won't remember the amount of dust on top of the telly when they are too small even to see the top of it. So, it's probably best to leave it and enjoy a nap instead.

I also needed to apply the 'being relaxed' principle to my expectations of Sundays. Whereas I'd previously been leading services and involved in all sorts of up-front stuff in our little congregation in Singapore, and at other times able to concentrate fully on the songs or the sermon, now I was confined to holding the baby, feeding the baby, changing the baby and taking the baby out of earshot. But rather than stay at home, I tried to make church a priority. I wanted to set the arrow to the mark and make Sunday church a rhythm that we stuck to as a family. I knew that I would benefit from the parts of the service I could participate in, even if I couldn't be there for the whole time. And I knew that our church family would be encouraged to see the newest member. And to see me too, even with baby sick over my cardie and big unsightly black bags under my eyes.

I do love being a mum, but parenthood has also been the means of repeatedly exposing sin in my heart. And right from when my daughter was a newborn baby, I came to recognize my need to find daily grace from God. The first few weeks with a new baby contain very little routine, and finding a moment even to bring to mind the grace of God seems a vast task. Here is another place where a relaxed attitude can help. A brief Bible verse and a thoughtful run-through of the Lord's Prayer is a devotional routine. Or mindful singing along with Christian music or the reading of an encouraging Christian biography which you can actually concentrate on, whereas a more doctrinal book would make your brain feel like blancmange. It might not be the chunky quiet time I used to have, but it is something. And something's always better than nothing.

Once a routine is established (it does happen, eventually, honestly), kids are a great alarm clock, especially in the early years. And prayer and Bible reading, even a single verse, snatched while semi-comatose with a breastfeeding baby, is better than waiting for a perfect moment for a perfect quiet time. Technology can be a great help in the years of sleeplessness. The Daily Bible App provides a verse a day to take with me. My mobile phone can read the Bible to me out loud. Being creative with my devotional life has enabled me to keep on going with God. I'm a sucker for new materials, and, although a new book or method won't fix the sinful heart that would rather sleep or read a novel, each new thing helps me to refocus. Even if it's left half-done in the end, it's still worthwhile. A parent who's spoken and listened to God half the time intended is better for my children than one who's completely ignored the Creator, Sustainer and Redeemer of all.

Messy infants

Once children start to stay awake for a while, then sit up, then crawl, toddle and talk, new challenges will arise. The exhaustion remains, but added to it is the new component to parenting: the anxiety of raising the children, of helping them hit the mark we're aiming at. How can I show my child how to glorify God? As it dawned on me that the small person now in my life was different from me but was going to rely on me to learn how to negotiate the world, I started reading every parenting book going. And although most of them had useful tips, no one book ever covered all I felt I needed to know.

In Deuteronomy, the key advice for parents is to infuse all life with God's Word:

> You shall love the LORD your God with all your heart and with
> all your soul and with all your might. And these words that I
> command you today shall be on your heart. You shall teach them
> diligently to your children, and shall talk of them when you sit in
> your house, and when you walk by the way, and when you lie
> down, and when you rise.
> (Deuteronomy 6:5–7)

This is a pretty messy way of doing things. It's not about set times for Bible study with the kids or regular family devotions, good and useful though these are. It's about talking about God and his Word when we're lounging about watching telly or walking to school or snuggling in bed in the holidays or eating supper or driving to swimming lessons. It's about gossiping God in the normal everyday things, relating life to God and God to life. This is what God's people are called to do; it's his method for reaching the next generation.

When my kids were infants, in school nursery and Key Stage 1, reading occupied many of our hours. This was when I did most reading to the kids and when I started helping them to learn to read for themselves. The first words my younger son learnt to read were: 'God' (yay for us) and 'Dave' (not so yay). This was because his favourite Bible reading book at the time was that classic of children's Christian literature: the *Veggie Tales Bible Storybook*. And his particularly favourite story in that book was Dave and the Giant Pickle (David and Goliath adapted for vegetables, of course). Imagining Goliath as a giant gherkin when he was three has not had a hugely detrimental effect on his theological development, I am relieved to tell you. He loved the story, loved to read it and hear about God, notwithstanding the vegetable content.

That was the stage when my children were learning lots of new things. A popular activity was swimming, and one school holiday I'd booked my daughter, aged about five, into a week of lessons. What on earth possessed me to commit to swimming lessons at 9am in the holidays? I really don't know. So, of course, we were leaving with no time to spare one morning, and the phone rang.

I was planning to leave it to ring out, but my daughter had just learnt to answer phones so she had other ideas. She wasn't being very coherent, but, as I thought it was my mother, I simply asked my daughter to hand over the phone. Loudly and directly, as my daughter was rather caught up in the excitement of being on the phone, and because I was anxious to leave for swimming. Eventually, I got hold of the receiver and, thankfully, before I'd flapped at my mother, I realized it was the bishop calling to speak to my husband. Oh dear. Cue: a teaching session on asking, 'Who's calling?' when playing receptionist.

Since young children are such sponges, learning poems, songs and stories by heart, this is a great age at which to start absorbing memory verses and Christian songs. It was also the age when our own children learnt the habits of confession and forgiveness. We wanted them to learn to say more than, 'Sorry', so we also taught the child who was on the receiving end of an apology to say, 'I forgive you'. A two-way reconciliation is always better than just an apology on its own. They have learnt to mirror God's forgiveness, which isn't just an 'it's OK; it doesn't matter', but instead an understanding that forgiveness is costly but right. Sometimes the forgiveness for an offence takes a while to be offered, but 'I forgive you' will always come eventually.

Top tips from the vicarage: Kid's Bibles from the vicarage collection

This is not a complete list. We have tried many different kids' Bibles and lots of different Bible story books, and this is a sample of some I remember using more regularly than others and ones which are currently popular. We always found that the more, the merrier. Most of what the kids have learnt from these Bibles has not only come through the stories themselves, but from the way we have read and discussed them together. An added bonus of reading the Bible with your child is that this can actually be a part of your own devotional routine too. As I read Bible stories with my kids, I was myself focusing on God. As kids grow older, they will still love to read the simpler story Bibles, and enjoy reading them to younger siblings too.

1. **For babies and toddlers:** We used Bible story books with very short, clear stories:
   - *The God Loves Me Bible* by Susan Beck[2] – every story ends with 'and God loves ME!'
   - *The Rhyme Bible Storybook for Toddlers* by L. J. Sattgast and Toni Goffe[3] – lots of fun to read aloud
   - *The Beginners' Bible for Toddlers* by Catherine DeVries and Kelly Pulley[4]

2. **For infants:** We used a mix of fun stories and great illustrations:
   - *The Beginners' Bible.*[5] Use it with *Beginning with God* Bible notes for young children.
   - *The Big Picture Story Bible* by David Helm.[6] The pictures in this book are very clever – look carefully to see more than just simple illustrations of the story.
   - *The Veggie Tales Bible Storybook* by Cindy Kenney and Big Idea Design.[7] This includes Bible text from the New International Readers' Version, so it's not all Dave and the Giant Pickle.

- *The Rhyme Bible Storybook* by Linda Sattgast.[8] All kids love poems, so this a fun way to share Bible stories. With a rhyming story, you may find some will stick for life.
- *The Lion Storyteller Bible* by Bob Hartman and Krisztina Kállai Nagy.[9] You can get this with a great CD set too, but we found it was, alas, too exciting for my daughter to fall asleep to.

3. **For juniors and tweens:**

- *International Children's Bible*[10] used with *XTB* Bible reading notes. This Bible is a special translation with children in mind, using simple vocabulary. The Bible reading notes are lots of fun, with quizzes and games and clear application for 8–11s.
- *The Jesus Storybook Bible* by Sally Lloyd-Jones[11] – beautifully told stories with gorgeous illustrations, highlighting how the whole Bible story points to Jesus
- *My First Message* by Eugene H. Peterson[12] – devotional Bible with short extracts from *The Message* version together with questions to think about and suggestions for prayer and application
- *The Gospel Story Bible* by Marty Machowski[13] – lots of stories and lots of connections to show how God's plan of salvation is fulfilled throughout Scripture
- *The Action Bible* by Doug Mauss and Sergio Cariello[14] – graphic-novel style, well told, with fantastic illustrations. Currently being enjoyed by our eight-year-old son. We don't have the CDs, but there are some available. There is also a devotional book with stories from this Bible.

Messy juniors

The day comes when we find that the kids can dress themselves and are reading unaided. They are firmly expressing preferences about everything: music, TV programmes, family activities, yoghurt flavours, whatever. They are in the Juniors at school, or Key Stage 2 as it's now known, and it seems that by now you're assumed to have this whole parenting thing sussed. All the sympathy and help so kindly given when kids are tiny and prone to sicky bugs rather peters out when they are stropping and arguing back and needing to get homework done or tidy their bedrooms.

Interestingly, I have found it much harder to deal with a child not wanting to clear up a few books or some dirty clothes than one who vomits right through the night. And there is endless worry about whether or not there's any truth in the saying attributed to the Jesuits: 'Give me the child until he is seven and I'll give you the man.' I can see that my children's personalities have manifested themselves now that they are eleven, ten and eight, but I'm praying that not all their character traits are fixed irrevocably, and that they will be redeemed by God's grace, which clothes us 'with power to do what is right'.

I have found Sundays to be a particular challenge at this age. Of course, as I've said before, in a vicarage, children are absolutely guaranteed to misbehave on Sunday mornings. It comes with their dad's dog collar. Once Daddy is out of the door to the early service or has just left for the main service, they unleash their inner terrors. If I was organized and on top of life, I would surely have an exciting activity up my sleeve and be waiting to occupy these bouncing-about children, but I rarely manage that. So, I need to pray my way through those Sunday mornings, seeking God's grace and trusting his providence. I can remember that his power is made perfect in weakness (2 Corinthians 12:9) and I can seek his forgiveness for my part in the mess. And I will try hard to make less of a hash of it next week.

Messy music

How do you get kids to walk home from school when they're small and complaining about the distance? There's the 'win-you' technique, where you 'race' them to the next lamp post or get them to 'race' each other. Everyone wins, of course, and gets a cheer when they get there. And then there's the singing technique. The favourite song to speed us home from school when my kids were smaller was one we'd learnt at toddler group:

> I am a sheep (baa baa) and I like to be well fed.
> I am a sheep (baa baa), a little stupid in the head.
> I go astray most every day, what a trouble I must be.
> I'm glad I've got the Good Shepherd looking after me
>   (ah-ah-ah-ah-BAA-BAA).
> (Anon.)

The loud shouts of 'baaing' were always effective in lifting little feet, as my flock wended its way home through the distinctly unpastoral landscape of terraced houses and busy roads.

Christian songs have been at the heart of our family soundtrack since I painfully taught myself to play 'How Deep the Father's Love for Us'[15] on the piano when I was pregnant with my daughter. Since my last piano lesson had been about sixteen years previously and I had failed my last exam, this was more challenging than it sounds.

We've taught them kids' songs and choruses and also tried to help them to learn richer hymns. Our middle son's favourite song is 'In Christ Alone',[16] which we sang to him as a lullaby most nights from when he was about six months old until when he was four or five.

When my daughter was small and we were still living in Singapore, a friend introduced me to the Australian writer of kids' songs, Colin Buchanan (not to be confused with the Anglican bishop). His songs are musically interesting, often amusing and theologically robust. We found his first couple of albums in Singapore and have been listening to them ever since, even attending his concerts every couple of years. We also sing Colin's songs in church and at school assemblies.

Before our older kids reached Year 5 at school, any music in the car was almost always Christian music, including Colin's stuff, but also Seeds Family Worship, Sovereign Grace Kids, Emu albums like *The King, The Snake and The Promise*, Ishmael's albums, Doug Horley's music and the Great Big God series. Now the kids are a bit older, we have to mix the music in the car up a bit, but our eight-year-old still listens to exclusively Christian music on his MP3 player.

Colin Buchanan, Ishmael and Seeds Family Worship have a great selection of Bible memory verses set to music. It's a great way to learn Scripture by heart, and grown-ups benefit too. We've tried many other methods for Bible verse memory, but the musical options definitely work best. We made up the setting of Philippians 2:14 (NCV) below ourselves:

> Do everything
> [This o-old man]
> wi-ithout
> [he played one]
> co-omplaining or arguing.
> [he played nick-nack on my-y thumb]
> A-and that's from Philipp-i-ans two-oo verse fourteen
> [With a nick-nack p-paddywack, give a dog a bone]
> Ph'lippians two-oo verse fourteen.
> [this old man came rolling home]
> (Sung, just about, to the tune of 'This Old Man, He Played One')

There are so many good resources available and there's always something new on the market. YouTube and Spotify are great ways to test before buying. As our kids get older, we are dipping into WOW CDs, compilation albums of Christian music which cover a wide range of genres, so they work as good introductions. The other grown-up in our family is also a fan of LeCrae's rap, while I love Andrew Peterson's gentle folk (his 'Matthew's Begats' is a family favourite). The kids are beginning to listen to those too. In our own messy way, we continue to pour God's Word into our family life and trust it to do its valuable work in all our hearts.

Messy tweens and teens

My husband and I are only tentatively beginning to venture into this area of parenting, although we have both led youth groups and summer ventures with teenagers for years, so we know this age group pretty well. It's rather less stressful being a youth leader than the parent, although leading youth groups can certainly have its downsides too. The families and community worker at our church always likes to look on the bright side after a youth group session. If nothing's been set on fire and no-one's died, then, hooray, we have things to be thankful for.

Paul Tripp's book *Age of Opportunity* challenges the idea that parenting teenagers is about surviving the turbulence of hormones. He rightly highlights the great challenge that, as teenagers begin to express their own personalities more clearly, not only are their hearts exposed, but our own hearts are laid bare and we increasingly see our own wrong thoughts and desires. He says, 'God knows our weakness. He is aware of our sin. And he has given us glorious gifts of grace so that we can be his tools of change in our children's lives.'[17]

Our need of grace is made very clear to us by children who can see our sin and name it. This is why (another) Paul wrote, 'Fathers, do not provoke your children to anger, but bring them up in the discipline and instruction of the Lord' (Ephesians 6:4). Anger is an easy emotion to provoke, especially when hunger and tiredness come into play. We see more of it than we'd like in the first hour or so after the end of the school day. And that's just from the parents. I need grace to let go of angry thoughts without needing to express them. I need grace to hear the anger expressed by my children without escalating the situation.

As I mentioned earlier, my daughter began secondary school last year. In the first term and a half, she lost a jumper, two bus passes and a mobile phone. And she lost one of her school shoes for a whole fortnight before it was recovered. Now, her entire PE kit appears to be missing too. Every time she has a clarinet lesson, I pray the instrument back home through the front door. (She has an aunt who, in the course of her school career, managed to lose two flutes by leaving them on public transport, so there is family form in this regard.) Every time she comes home having lost something is an opportunity for us to show grace to her and help her trust in God's providence. It will be harder if it's the clarinet that goes AWOL, but, if we're thinking right, lost things can remind us of our own lostness and the joy of being found. I can't tell you how relieved we were when the lost shoe turned up. Indeed, there was much rejoicing in the vicarage. My daughter's appearance at school in trainers had been noted by the headmistress, and I had received a call from the head of year. The first year of secondary school in our house has often seemed like an illustration package for Jesus' parables of lostness: not a coin but a shoe, not a sheep but a schoolbook.

We like to share our kids and their messiness with others as much as possible, and, now that they are headed for secondary school, youth groups and summer ventures have come into play. My daughter is increasingly wanting to talk about faith with her youth leader rather than her parents. Over the years, our ministry trainee lodgers have taken on parental roles too, although, as the kids grow older, they are turning more into older brothers. As our tweens and teens grow and begin to question their parents' wisdom, we are trying to ensure that they spend time with other Christian adults who can model faith differently from the way we do it. We want them to see that our sins do not define our faith – indeed, we pray that they will see beyond our poor models to the perfect Lord Jesus. Other Christians can help our children see Christ in ways that we don't reflect him. Children of all ages never fit into neat-and-tidy categories, and so our parenting never can either. Messy kids need messy parenting: flexible and prepared to change and do things differently.

Messy devotions with kids

When time has been set aside for family devotions, one or all of the following are guaranteed to occur at the exact moment the Bible is opened: loud meowing from the cat, a child who needs the loo, the remembrance of extremely important homework needing to be done immediately, a phone call from a churchwarden/funeral director/parishioner with a major crisis, or repeated rings of the doorbell by children wanting bike tyres pumped up. Well, that's how it seems in our house anyway.

As our kids have changed and grown and their routines have altered, the ways we have prayed with them have changed too. When they were small, we'd read the Bible with each child individually and pray with them too. We must have got through about twenty different children's Bibles (some of which you met earlier) in our journey through the infancy of three children. Some were gifts, but mostly, we bought them ourselves. We often found the kids became stale with a single format of study book, so we mixed them all up, from more serious and wordy kids' Bibles to less accurate but more fun versions. What we felt was important was that our kids were excited to hear the stories, and that they heard them told in different ways so that Bible truths were stored in their hearts. And we missed some nights and occasionally had to change books halfway through, after the one we were using went sadly missing among the debris.

Now that our children are bigger, we encourage them to read the Bible for themselves, and we provide Bible reading notes or books of devotions if they want them. We're also beginning to have family devotions more frequently, since they can all now read and concentrate for more than a nanosecond. With a household that's in and out for after-school activities, we can't manage to be together every night, but, remembering that doing something is always better than doing nothing, we persevere in the time available. Our usual hit rate seems to be only once a week, but lately we've been making a concerted effort to manage more than that. We are particularly enjoying *Thoughts to Make Your Heart Sing* by Sally Lloyd-Jones just now. Sometimes, devotions mean ploughing on through refusals to read and bickerings and interruptions involving someone being sent to the stairs to contemplate their behaviour. God, in his grace and providence, can use messy devotions to work in all our hearts. Most importantly, we're taking the opportunities to talk about God's Word with our children. Messy or not, we can trust God that his Word will do his work.

Messy grown kids

Having grown kids is a parenting stage we are still anticipating, but, being an adult child myself, I see much truth in the description I once heard of parenting as 'thirteen years of exhaustion followed by a lifetime of worry'.

The Lord Jesus tells his people not to be anxious about tomorrow (Matthew 6:34), so my aim is to get past the sleeplessness and start to learn to let the Lord deal with tomorrow. Grown-up children obviously mark the end of the intensive parenting years. We have been aiming them at the mark of God's glory and the service of their generation. Now we release our arrows, trusting God for the future.

It's clearly not the end of parenting when the kids leave home: I still turn to my parents for advice (and even poems – see the beginning of this book). Leaving home well is the goal of parenting, but not a stage I am looking forward to as a parent. For now, I bear this stage in mind because I need to prepare for it now if we're going to be ready for it when it comes. So, I teach my kids about the messiness of life by talking and walking God's Word as much as possible through my own mess and sinfulness. I try new things when old routines stop working. I make a mess of things and ask my children for forgiveness. I set my eyes on the mark of God's glory and trust his grace to get me there.

Grace and providence in parenting

A parenting seminar I once attended had a great line that we were urged to stick up on our mirrors or inside our kitchen cupboards: 'You are a model.' This is an especially good line to remember when I've struggled out of bed sleep-deprived with unwashed hair! It's true though. I may not be glamorous, but as a parent I am a model of Christian faith to my children. I'm also, scarily, as I've said, a model of sinful patterns of behaviour to my children. So, I need to know how to model grace and forgiveness when that sin occurs, as it surely will.

I'm still aiming the arrow to the mark as I ask my son's forgiveness following a disagreement badly handled. Here, I can model grace for him. I also need grace to forgive the kids when they sin against me. I'm talking about God as I sit down weeping after a row, and I'm talking about his Word as we reflect on the sin of today and pray our teatime confession together.

I could spend a lot of time worrying about my kids' future. Will they finish their homework this week? Will they be picked for the school team next term? Will they keep reading their Bibles when they turn into teenagers? Will they make friends at their new school? Will they follow Christ when they leave home? None of these outcomes is guaranteed, of course. But, when things look like they are going wrong, I need to remember God's providence: his good ordering of his world in every circumstance.

The Scottish Presbyterian minister Ebenezer Erskine reminds us how grace and providence work together 'for [our] benefit and advantage':

> First, A word of consolation. Know then, believer, for thy comfort, that 'the holy One of Israel is thy King, and in his favour thy horn shall be exalted; mercy and truth shall go before his face,' with a special view to thy happiness in time and through eternity. All the grace and mercy that is in the heart of the King, is ordained for thee, and secured to thee by a well ordered covenant. The whole of his administrations, whether of grace or of providence, are calculated for thy benefit and advantage, Rom. 8:28. You are the children of the King; he has adopted thee into his family, yea, settled an inheritance upon thee, as 'heirs of God, and joint heirs with himself.'[18]

I have been given children not only for their benefit, but by the King who has a special view to my happiness in time and throughout eternity. This is a truth I need to grasp with all my heart as I stumble messily through motherhood, falteringly but with determination, setting arrows at the mark of God's glory.

5. messy church

Today I missed out one of the Ten Commandments. (Murder, since you ask).
I drank up all the consecrated wine with two communicants still to go.
The readings did not correspond with the preacher's sermon.
The CD player wouldn't work. So someone went to get another one. Which arrived after the first hymn. And then the CD kept sticking or skipping or something.
So, a typical service.
Everyone seemed happy and edified![1]

Have you ever been to a church service like that, as described by Sussex parson Marc Lloyd? I've been to plenty. More than plenty. When fallen people run a gathering of fallen people, there are limitless opportunities for mess. And not all of them are down to a failure of technology, although projector systems, computers and microphones can always be relied on to provide entertaining slip-ups. But Marc's church members were still happy and edified, despite the mess. How does that happen? And how can we help, as members, to make church a happy and edifying community, outside the regular gatherings as well as in them, despite all the mess?

Messy church services remind us of the relationships that make up a church family. Church services can be messy on purpose – we hold a monthly Messy Church[2] for families – but, more frequently, messiness is accidental. Let's face it, church life is never straight-forward. People keep on messing up plans for what is meant to be happening. The computer fails or the microphones howl. People forget to come and take their turn to serve refreshments after the service. Occasionally, disturbed or drunken people shout out during the prayers. Vicarage children refuse to sit where their mother asks them to sit. What's going wrong?

What is church?

In the New Testament, the word 'church' (*ekklesia* in Greek) is used to refer to all believers: the worldwide church, and to gatherings of believers: the local church. There is much encouragement in the worldwide church, but also too much mess for me to cover in this chapter, so I want to concentrate on the local church.

Saints, sinners, services

The local church is primarily a gathering of sinners who are also saints. Messy sinful saints meet for Sunday services and at other times throughout the week. And local churches tend to reflect their local areas. I've been a member of a traditional suburban Anglican church, of large churches with high proportions of students, of a church in a country where significant sections of the population were forbidden to become Christians, of a church where the main congregation worshipped in a language other than English and, more recently, I've attended two small churches in deprived multicultural areas. What have I discovered? Church is pretty much the same wherever you go. The flavour of the sin among the saints may differ a bit, after-service refreshments might vary between biscuits and cake or rambutans (hairy lychees much loved in South East Asia) and string hoppers (rice noodles fried together to make small pancakes – delicious with curry), but, wherever there are saints and services in which they meet together, the differences are far fewer than you might imagine.

In a recently published book, I came across this definition of the local church: 'The primary place where the Kingdom of Heaven impacts the kingdoms of this world.'[3] If the kingdom of heaven is impacting the kingdoms of this world, it is no surprise at all that we will find mess in our local church. The kingdoms of this world will be fighting for supremacy and encouraging the mayhem that arises from our sinfulness. The local church is where God chooses to impact the world. However small and insignificant it may be, it is where it's at in the plans of God.

Messy buildings, messy bodies, messy families, messy brides?

In the New Testament, we see the church described as a building. And not a finished building, all sparkly and ready for the dignitaries to cut the opening ribbon, but a building site:

> So then you are no longer strangers and aliens, but you are fellow
> citizens with the saints and members of the household of God, built
> on the foundation of the apostles and prophets, Christ Jesus himself
> being the cornerstone, in whom the whole structure, being joined
> together, grows into a holy temple in the Lord. In him you also are
> being built together into a dwelling place for God by the Spirit.
> (Ephesians 2:19–22)

I used to work as an engineer, designing water and sewage treatment works. On a couple of occasions, I spent stints on site, supervising installations of designs I had worked on. My longest placement was spent building a sewage screening plant in Inverness. We worked on a site by the River Ness where we installed pipework, concrete channels and screens inside a huge tin shed. I never wore smart clothes to work – I wore jeans, steel-toecapped boots and a hard hat. It was a building site, and we dressed accordingly, expecting to encounter mud and dust alongside the technical challenges. A building is not erected cleanly or easily. The reason I was working on site was precisely because the company knew that someone would be needed to sort out the design problems that would be encountered as equipment was installed.

When we build a church, there will be problems as the structure grows. Things may not fit together properly to start with, but God is still building his people in and through the mess.

Another New Testament way to describe the church is as a body (1 Corinthians 12), reminding us that churches are complex, and consist of very different parts which don't always work as they should do. Not everyone is connected into the body as strongly as they might be, but, as we grow our relationships in church, the body joins together, and muscles, tendons and sinews are exercised and developed. I'm not a big fan of exercise, partly because it's hard work. It's painful. And, of course, I'd always much rather be reading a book on the sofa. But I know that exercise is good for me, so I should do some. I really ought to strengthen my muscles, a great way to stave off the lower back pain that plagues me from time to time. In fact, I even joined a gym this week. And I'll be going along just as soon as I've finished writing this book. And tidying the house. And writing a few blog posts. And run out of excuses.

Some church muscle growth is painful. My sister's church changes round their small groups regularly. The change is hard, as people who meet together weekly now see one another less frequently. But when my sister was ill recently, we saw the power of the connections built in different small groups. The pain of change had brought about growth and strength in the body, and support to my sister and her family when they needed it.

The instruction to treat fellow believers as fathers and mothers, brothers and sisters (1 Timothy 5) reminds us that a church is also a family. We don't need reminding about the mess that a family is and causes. The local church family I am a part of is the people 'God has given me to love'. There may be good reasons to move church, but, if I'm finding my church family hard to love, I may just need to remember that God has given them to me to do just that. Once, I was told that, if I was finding a fellow Christian hard to love, the best thing to do would be to bake a cake for that person. Doing something practical for someone can grow my love for them. (NB: Don't worry if I've baked you a cake – it's not my usual reason for baking.)

In Revelation 19, the church is described as a bride. Although my floral headdress kept slipping around on my wedding day, I don't think I could have been described as a mess. Of course, the bride in Revelation is the church at the marriage feast of the Lamb. This is the church at the end of days, perfected and ready to meet the Lord. This is the time when we'll look back and see God's providence in putting us in the local church we were members of. This is when all we will see will be God's grace, and the mess of church life will be made perfect.

Top tips: Church buildings

1. **Be prepared:** Essential building work will always have to be carried out when the church is needed for major events, such as a visit from the bishop, Advent Christingle service, etc. Last time, our chancel was swathed in plastic sheeting covering over unsightly repairs to plasterwork.

2. **Signage:** All churches have an ancient blackboard easel somewhere. Do not be tempted to throw this out in a fit of tidiness because the Sunday school no longer uses it. It will shortly be needed to direct people to the side entrance when the front doors have to be cordoned off because of falling masonry.

3. **Electricity/gas meter readers:** These people will almost always call at the vicarage on The Day Off (a working day for most people, just not vicars) and require guiding through a maze of locked doors to the meters. Once you have ensured that they come on a more convenient day, you will find that the power supply contract is up for renewal, so you switch to a different supplier, and they turn up on The Day Off. Can't win.

4. **Missing items:** There are monsters living in the boiler room that come out at night and consume the following: tea towels, teaspoons, the reading glasses left by congregation members on the shelf at the back of the church and also the red fruit squash used as an alcohol-free alternative to communion wine.
5. **Squirrels:** If your church building becomes infested with squirrels, it is recommended that they be baptized as soon as possible. That will ensure that they will only return for services at Christmas and, occasionally, Easter.

Messy saints

The main thing that makes a local church messy is the presence of the messy saints who comprise it. Letters to the churches in the New Testament remind us that relational messes in congregations are nothing new. The church at Corinth is a good example: there was quarrelling (1 Corinthians 1:11) and a scandalous affair (1 Corinthians 5:1); people were taking each other to court (1 Corinthians 6) and getting drunk when celebrating the Lord's Supper (1 Corinthians 11:20–21), and they needed to be reminded that their services should have some sort of order (1 Corinthians 14).

When Paul anticipates a visit to Corinth, he has concerns about what he might find:

> For I fear that perhaps when I come I may find you not as I wish, and that you may find me not as you wish – that perhaps there may be quarrelling, jealousy, anger, hostility, slander, gossip, conceit, and disorder. I fear that when I come again my God may humble me before you, and I may have to mourn over many of those who sinned earlier and have not repented of the impurity, sexual immorality, and sensuality that they have practised.
> (2 Corinthians 12:20–21)

There are many reminders here of what we all find among saints in churches everywhere. Hopefully, the mess in our churches may not be as bad as in one church I know, where (I was told) a previous vicar had once been confronted by an angry church member wielding a machete at a particularly tense meeting. However, we should not be surprised by tensions and disagreements, part of the impact made as the kingdom of heaven meets the kingdoms of this world.

Because our local area is very culturally diverse, we are, unsurprisingly, finding increasing diversity among our church members too. So now, we have people not only from the more long-term white, Caribbean and Asian communities, but we are gradually being joined by Eastern Europeans and Africans who have moved into our area. This can make for messy cultural misunderstandings and blunders, but it also shows us the great need for grace in our relationships and reminds us all of our identity as 'sojourners and exiles' (1 Peter 2:11) in this world. None of us, if we are Christians, is truly at home where we live. Being among people of another culture is a very helpful reminder of this.

We have friends whose central London congregation has a 30% turnover every year. So, they deal with a messy scramble as people leave and home group leaders and members of the coffee rota have to be constantly replaced. They have a congregation of sojourners who are always on the move. In our parish, many people live in rented accommodation and, if a better house becomes available, they often move. Mess is generated by changes in relationships, the loss of friends and the hard work of getting to know newcomers. This is why every church needs to learn to be a church gladly prepared to accept the pain of change.

If our church looks messy because of the number of new faces or because people don't look or dress like one another, this is a reflection of the kingdom. We see all being changed from one degree of glory into another (2 Corinthians 3:18), and this will be the case until we all look like Christ as we enter the Father's presence at the end of days. Change is a reflection of God's grace to us – making us ready to meet him. And it's a part of his providence, ordering our world for his glory.

Messy services and messy meetings

The church where my husband and I got married boasted a large congregation with a wonderful music team and excellent Bible teaching. Everything ran smoothly almost all the time as staff and congregation worked hard to present the gospel both to believers and to the many enquirers who attended each week. But even when so many contingencies were made for things to run smoothly, there could still be hitches. Sometimes, an interruption would occur on a sweltering summer evening, when the doors of our city-centre building had been left open, and a chap somewhat the worse for wear would wander in. There might then be a pause in the usually seamless flow of the service while the visitor tried to contribute loudly to the sermon, before being encouraged to drink a cup of tea by the ever-vigilant church wardens.

At our current church, I often find it very hard to concentrate in the service because I'm anticipating all the things that might go wrong. In our four years in the parish, we've seen technical failures of all sorts (speakers, microphones, computer, video) and operator errors on the sound desk and projection software, especially when one of my adventurous children wants to get involved. There have been countless typos in songs and liturgy, where the in-house proofreader (me) has not got her act together on a Saturday evening. We've forgotten milk for the tea and coffee (usually rectified by me dashing home and getting ours – obviously why vicarages are built next door to churches). The other week my husband came home and grabbed a couple of pieces of bread from the top of our loaf for communion. Only when he came to break the bread in the service did he realize that those two slices had in fact been buttered.

And of course, there are the people, sometimes even including vicarage inhabitants, who've not turned up when scheduled to serve coffee, or arrived late, or turned up drunk or begging or arguing or demonstrating unforgiveness. What a mess. What a failure. But none of this is a surprise to the God who says he will build his church (Matthew 16:18). This outpost of the kingdom of God is where we catch glimpses of glory. There is so much mess, but sometimes things go smoothly. More often than not, we see kindness shown among the saints on a Sunday and during the week. We see a portion of God's character in his people. This is why we stick with the mess.

When we meet with God's people on a Sunday or another day, we don't just come to meet with a bunch of sinners. We come to meet saints – and our holy God. I need to remind myself that I'm not just getting together with fifty or so fallen and broken people, but that our meeting is reflected in the heavens:

> But you have come to Mount Zion and to the city of the living God, the heavenly Jerusalem, and to innumerable angels in festal gathering, and to the assembly of the firstborn who are enrolled in heaven, and to God, the judge of all, and to the spirits of the righteous made perfect, and to Jesus, the mediator of a new covenant, and to the sprinkled blood that speaks a better word than the blood of Abel.
> (Hebrews 12:22–24)

And of course, Sunday morning church services aren't all there is to church. We meet during the week too, so opportunities for mess also abound from Monday till Saturday. Our church hall has a kitchen. But who has all the tea towels? Where did they go? And who used up the butter I left in the fridge last week? Grace is so often what we need.

Grace and providence in church

I know I've mentioned it before, but Sunday mornings are not always my greatest hour. I often arrive at church in a tizzy of Sunday lunch preparation, child mediation and chivvying, and last-minute forgetfulness. Have I got all the materials for junior church? Did I put the oven on as well as the timer for the roast? Often, grace is far from my mind as I take my place while still trying to locate my children, who have scattered themselves around the building just as the notices are beginning.

An advantage of being Anglican is that our liturgy always involves a confession early on in the service. And there's always something I need to confess that has occurred in the brief time between rising and making it into the building. Seeking God's grace and forgiveness should help me, but still distractions plague me. Can I be gracious to the computer operator who keeps on missing the verse changes? Can I be gracious to my husband about his sermon? Am I failing to remember that, in meeting with the saints, I have come to Mount Zion?

I should never forget: these are the people God has given me to love. Twice, Peter has to tell his readers to love one another earnestly (1 Peter 1:22; 4:8). It's not obvious. It's not even easy. But I am to do it. I am to love people who are kind and gracious to me, and I'm also to love those who fail to love me back. It's much easier to love fellow believers at a distance: the struggling Christians we hear about in distant lands. The true challenge for me in church this Sunday is to love the person who is hard to love because of the way they treat me, or their unlovely attitude towards others in the congregation or community. We know one another here. And still, we are called to love one another. Earnestly. From a pure heart. So, I need to seek that pure heart which comes with God's forgiveness and grace.

More than that, we are called to show grace to one another in practical ways. I don't only need to forgive that person from the inside, but I'm to do good to them. I might need to invite them over for tea. But I might need to do something more costly still. If someone is of the household of faith, I am called to serve them especially: 'So then, as we have opportunity, let us do good to everyone, and especially to those who are of the household of faith' (Galatians 6:10).

The mess in my church family is simply a mirror of the mess inside my heart. As God changes my heart and the hearts of fellow church members, we ought to begin to see a difference. Am I looking for signs of God's grace changing hearts in my church? When grace gets a grip on hearts, we can soon see the difference. In one church, some people didn't come to take the Lord's Supper as they didn't feel 'good enough' to share the communion meal. As their understanding of grace grew, so did their confidence in the Lord and not themselves. They were then able to come to the table to be encouraged by the means that Jesus himself has provided.

The whole of the story of the church is a tale of God's providence, calling his people through the ages out of mess. Disputes and disagreements led to the spread of the gospel. Persecutions led to conversions. Paul and Silas's imprisonment and an earthquake brought salvation to the jailer at Philippi and his whole household (Acts 16). If things are a mess in our church family, we can still be sure that the Lord is the same God who changes things: 'For God, who said, "Let light shine out of darkness", has shone in our hearts to give the light of the knowledge of the glory of God in the face of Jesus Christ' (2 Corinthians 4:6).

If God can change my heart, he can change hearts in my church too. I want to seek to minimize my contribution to the mess as the Lord shines his light in my heart. And so I can play my part in doing good to God's people as we grow together into a holy temple, a dwelling place for God, by his Spirit.

Top tips: Kids in church

1. **Sunday school:** A mix-up with the Sunday school rota at least once a term is obligatory. It's a bit easier if everyone thinks they're on duty rather than no-one thinking it. Numbers that can vary between three and thirty (on a baptism Sunday) ensure that teachers are kept on their toes, and either there are not enough craft materials or else far too many that end up getting used as kindling for lighting the vicarage fire later.

2. **Refreshments:** It is much better to supply similar biscuits for all; the kids will always try to snaffle the chocolate ones. Don't be like the church we visited where the posh biscuits were served at one station only, far away from where the kids were leaving Sunday school, and the other station served Rich Tea fingers and

nothing else. Not a welcoming look. Learn to chill about the crumbs on the carpet. That's why we have a church hoover.

3. **Music:** Kids' songs are popular with 0–10s and 20–100s. Everyone in between will look a bit shuffly. Ignore this and do all the actions. If you give out shakers or tambourines, the grown-ups will want them too. Make sure you have enough to go round.

4. **Lost property:** All children will leave Sunday school crafts and their favourite hat behind in church most weeks. They won't remember about the craft, so just throw it away. The hat should be kept, however. It can join the reading glasses on the shelf at the back of the church.

5. **Messy Church:** A brilliant format for regular all-age services. Check out their website (www.messychurch.org.uk) for more details. Not to be confused with 'normal' church, which is *never* messy. Oh no.

6. Messy community

'You're the new vicar's wife, aren't you?'

I nodded, nervously. I'd just moved house. And community. And school gate. The old school gate was where I dropped my kids off, obviously, and also where I met my friends, chatted and laughed, and hung about until we were all thrown out by teachers wanting to get on with the lessons. At the new gate, I hung on to the kids for comfort and security. At the new school gate, I didn't know anyone. But some of them already knew me.

A mum came up to me, checked I was indeed married to the new minister, as above, and then told me about her social life: 'We went to see some strippers last night. But I was so drunk, I fell asleep and missed it.'

I wasn't very sure what she was expecting from me, but I commented, 'Sounds like a bit of an expensive way to take a nap.'

Then she wandered back to her 'gang'. I wasn't sure if I'd said the right thing, but it can't have been that bad, because she became my friend. I have to say though that I think this was rather a scary way to start life in a new place.

What's your community like? Did it welcome you with open arms when you moved there? Or, maybe you've always lived there. Does everyone know you or hardly anyone? How do you think about your neighbours? Our church has a mission statement that includes the aim to 'bless the people [of West Bromwich] by hearing, receiving and joyfully living out the gospel of Jesus Christ together'.

Blessing the people around us is part of what we are called to do as Christians, and ultimately blessing them by sharing the gospel of Jesus Christ. I'm sure you realize that this is a rather roundabout way of talking about evangelism. That scary thing that Christians avoid because of the embarrassment factor. You know. Talking about Jesus. And it isn't just embarrassing but it can get messy too. Because every community is made up of messy people, and the Christians who are supposed to be bringing the blessing can make such a hash of things. Good thing that it's God who's the One who calls us to make disciples, and his grace is available and his providence is already in action.

What is community?

There are lots of proper academic definitions of community, but since you hear phrases that vary from 'the local community' to 'the online gaming community' to 'the Punjabi community', the best I think we can say is that a community is a group of people somehow linked together. And those links can be forged through many aspects of life: geography, work, country of origin, language, social activities, a school, and so on, and most people are part of more than one community. Increasingly, some communities are to be found online.

There may be an element of choice in my membership of most of the communities I am a part of, perhaps because I've chosen where to live or work or send my kids to school, or I've chosen to join a particular running club or choir. And pretty much every community I belong to will include people I didn't choose to be connected to – wouldn't have chosen to be connected to if I had realized! If I live somewhere, I am naturally part of a local community. I may have chosen to live in that area, but I won't have chosen all my neighbours. Similarly, I might have had a choice of jobs, but I haven't chosen who sits at the next desk. Or, I might have thoroughly investigated the local primary schools, but I have pretty much no say in who I'm going to be bumping into at the school gate. The other runners in my club or the tenors in the choir might be fun, like-minded and easy to hang out with. Or they might be a cause of anxiety, angst and stress.

If Christians and churches (which are, of course, communities in themselves) are called to bless and bring the gospel to their wider communities, we need to think how we can best do this when communities are messy and so too is our blessing and our bringing. One of the ways a church can do this is by modelling community to those on the fringes and further afield. Individual Christians and families can do it too – interaction with our wider community is how we develop the relationships where we share Christ.

Our town is fairly small, although part of a large conurbation. There's still a strong sense of place, and not many people have cars. Not many members of our congregation are in work, as many have retired. Those people who do work have colleagues who are also strongly linked to their locality. It's the same with people who are members of social clubs or similar – local ties are strong. Few people travel far. So, at our church we try and concentrate our evangelism on local activities for local people. Our community is mostly linked by geography, hence our localized mission statement. Family fun days and beetle drives are popular. And great for building relationships and meeting our neighbours.

I've been in churches where it's been so different. In other places, my community has included work colleagues or students or expatriates or other networks of people. A fish-and-chip supper with a beetle drive might not be the best way to go in every place, but the good news of God taking our mess on himself is always just the same.

Messy light
It's pretty easy to see the mess in my local area. We see physical mess in the rubbish in the churchyard. A few months ago, a bunch of kids brought in some old car wheels and broken plastic toys and great lumps of wood they'd found in a skip, aiming for some sort of scrap party. We see relational mess in arguments between neighbours that

spill out into the street, usually in the summer months. A neighbour recently called round carrying his tea on a plate, along with (rather randomly) an unopened tin of rice pudding, looking for some help in moving out. There'd been some sort of a row, and he'd been kicked out of the house mid-meal on a freezing evening in early spring.

In other places, physical mess is quickly cleared up, and broken relationships are hidden behind gates or long driveways or in glamorous lifestyles. We only see the relational mess in some neighbourhoods if there is a major breakdown in a family. But it's still there, behind the curtains even in the most grandiose households. We only have to glance at tabloid headlines to realize that relational mess is no respecter of wealth and privilege.

Jesus tells his followers that they are to be a light in a dark world:

> You are the light of the world. A city set on a hill cannot be hidden.
> Nor do people light a lamp and put it under a basket, but on a stand,
> and it gives light to all in the house. In the same way, let your light
> shine before others, so that they may see your good works and give
> glory to your Father who is in heaven.
> (Matthew 5:14–16)

How do we light the world when our light is covered with busy baskets of work and family, church life and heavy expectations? Has Jesus been hidden behind my desire to fit in? Am I saving my light for the mission next year when I'm going to help at that women's event? Do I need to cut some holes in my baskets? Do I need some help to get up onto a stand?

If I do good things in my community: babysit for my neighbour, help with painting someone's living room, give a choir member a lift home, volunteer to man the stall at the school fête or help a colleague who needs some extra input in a project, and people assume it's because I'm a good egg, then I've been using a basket. Jesus calls me to do these good deeds so that people will give glory to *God*. They won't do that if they have no idea what prompts my good deeds. So, I need to introduce the name of Jesus as soon as possible in my relationship with people. Not in a weird way, of course, but I need to become known as a believer.

I have the advantage of being known as a Christian in my community. Well, my faith is assumed because of my husband's job – not necessarily a wise connection to make. But it does mean that, when I am seen to do something that benefits the community, God gets some of the glory. It also means that, when I mess up, the reflection on God isn't too hot either. This is both an incentive to get things right and also a temptation to keep my head down in case I make a hash of it, which I so often do.

How do we light the world when our light is covered with busy baskets of work and family, church life and heavy expectations?

I'm a saint – and I'm also a sinner, and so I also need to ensure that people don't assume that I won't ever make a mess of things. I need to model grace in my relationships so that, when I need to be forgiven, as is very likely, it won't seem like an alien concept to those from whom I seek it. Sometimes, my light will be hidden by my sin, but seeking forgiveness and reconciliation will lift the basket that's covered it over.

But we can't make a mess of the relationships we don't have. Sometimes, we don't have much time to get to know people or to put ourselves in the way of people we don't know all that well. A friend who works full-time for a church deliberately joined a weekly evening class and a sports club because she didn't really know anyone other than church people. From those activities, she's made new friends and given herself the opportunity to be part of a community outside the church family. And to bring Christ's light to them.

Every Christian is commissioned by Jesus, sharing in the task he gave to the apostles: 'Go therefore and make disciples of all nations . . .' (Matthew 28:19). As you know, our parish is full of people from all nations. In fact, there were twenty-six languages spoken at home among the kids at the church school at the last count. People are moving in and out of the area all the time. But what a great opportunity! We don't need to go to the nations to make disciples of people from all over the place. And all neighbourhoods in the UK, especially urban ones, are increasingly multicultural. This means that Christians need to be increasingly equipped to reach out cross-culturally. And should expect to make more of a mess of things as we make cultural blunders.

Having been an expatriate, I know that an invitation to someone's home is the best way to welcome a person from another culture. Malaysia and Singapore have the great institution of inviting everyone you know to your home on festive occasions. In the vicarage, we hold 'open house' on Sunday afternoons from time to time. Tea and cake are very easy to serve and don't produce vast quantities of washing-up. You don't even need to do the baking yourself. And it's a great way of welcoming church and fringe and neighbours together. One friend who lives in a rather smart area was thanked for her open house and its relaxed nature by neighbours who were used to turning up to events where hired staff served the fancy offerings. Being in someone's home feels like a welcome into a family. And we mirror God's invitation into his family when we open our house to others.

There are great things about being in a community for the long haul. I'm loving the fact that we've been living here for four years now. That means I don't have to take everyone through *Two Ways to Live* the first time I meet them. Of course, as you get to know someone for the first time, there can indeed be good opportunities to share the gospel clearly, using an outline. But in the day-to-day, little-by-little growth of relationships in a community, the gospel can come along in little bits. My husband likes to use a Bible story that sheds light on a situation that's being discussed – he calls this a 'gospel bite'. Someone who's struggling with money issues might need to know that God cares for them and be encouraged from Matthew 6:25–34, or, if we're talking about feelings of dissatisfaction, we could talk about how Paul learnt to be content in all situations (Philippians 4). If we apply God's Word into our own lives, we can share gospel bites about how we've coped in struggles or been changed by God. If you sit down at our dining table, you'll see a sheet of reminders to the family about how we can live well together. The first verse is: 'If possible, so far as it depends on you, live peaceably with all' (Romans 12:18). It's a good discussion starter for anyone who's eating at our table, reminding us all that we need grace in our dealings with one another.

Grace to our community

Every community I'm a part of is a mess. I live in a neighbourhood, in a town; I have kids at schools; I tweet and have a Facebook account. I'm a school governor and a library user, a blogger and a vicar's wife. At some point in every community I'm a part of, I've seen fallings out and difficulties, misunderstandings and sin. I'm not surprised by the sin I see. Because every one of the people in those groups is a sinner, someone who needs God's grace.

As a mum of primary school kids, I find that school gates can be a hotbed of insecurity and tensions, as people recall their own school days and find themselves worried about being told off by the teachers. School-gate mums fall out with me, with one another, with the teachers, with their kids. I've seen some fallings out erupt rather spec-tacularly into fisticuffs or screaming matches. And not just at our school gate. At other school gates, the mess might be more subtle – someone doesn't return your texts, or your children are missed off a birthday party invitation. There's a cool distancing. But every community needs grace and people to model that grace. If we're Christians who know God's grace, who better to be models of forgiveness and help?

In some communities, fallings out can last for years, even spanning generations. Some friends of ours live in a parish in a former pit village. One Sunday, a chap came to church asking if the vicar was doing a funeral the following week. His dad had died and his siblings hadn't told him because he'd broken the strike. The miners' strike was twenty-five years ago, and bitterness had gripped that family for a quarter of a century. That is a community needing God's grace to break in. I'm glad my friends are there, telling people about Jesus and offering God's grace that can clothe us with power to do what is right.

Many people in our local community know about the homeless man who's lived on our doorstep on and off over the last four years, in between stints in prison and periods of being housed. His presence has often made a physical mess of our home: discarded chip packets and cider bottles in the flowerbed normally indicate his return before we actually see him face to face. His tendency to sing loudly on the front doorstep at 6am has also caused tempers in the vicarage to become somewhat frayed. You see, none of the vicarage inhabitants are early-morning people. And we've worried about him, because his health is dubious and he seems unable to settle in a home.

We sometimes lose patience with him. But usually, when he comes to church, which he often does, a good number of the congregation feel able to show him grace. They talk to him, feed him, heat up his Pot Noodle. He's forgiven for drunken outbursts and rudeness. He is loved. And so, the mess right on our doorstep is a means of God's grace being shown – in our family, in our church and in our neighbourhood. Not that we welcome the early-morning calls, you understand, but we can see God's grace working in us and in our doorstep friend.

Providence in community

Our churchyard has a small playground. It was built to bless the families who live around the church, especially those who attend our toddler group. And many families enjoy using it. However, the playground has also attracted other children too. It's lovely to see so many kids out and about in the summer. But they have often come along without grown-ups, and, once you get around eight or more children of junior school age or older together without adult supervision, I can predict that there will be some sort of problem. Sometimes, it's just a few sweetie wrappers dropped about the place. And the churchyard grass is looking pretty ragged these days because of the enthusiastic games of football played there. On bright evenings, sitting in our living room, we often hear high-pitched squealing that gives us all a headache. Once there was even a small fire that needed immediate adult attention.

Our blessing of families with play equipment has brought with it some chaos. But this mess also brings us increased opportunities to bless our neighbours with the gospel. If young people are being noisy in the churchyard in the evening or on a Sunday afternoon, my husband often makes time to go out and chat to them about eternal things. We figure that, if they listen, they'll be blessed, and, if they get fed up and go home, that's a blessing too! Once, when he went out to talk to some of the loud teenagers, they asked him straight: 'You're not going to talk to us about hell again are you?' A couple of those teenagers have recently been along to a course explaining the basics of the Christian faith. They may not be there yet with Jesus, but they're closer than they previously were. And the mess of the playground has been a part of that important journey.

Another minister we know was officially starting his new job. The special licensing service was being held, with the bishop, the local MP, clergy from the town, church members and other visitors all in attendance. The new vicar was about to speak towards the end of the ceremony. Suddenly, there was an interruption: the tinkling sound of windows breaking at the back of the church, showering the well-dressed, well-heeled visitors with shards of stained glass.

The teenage boys who'd been throwing stones were quickly apprehended by local police. They were also spoken to by the bishop and by their head teacher, who was, incidentally, attending the service. Following on from the glass breaking, the new vicar was able to visit the families of the boys concerned, and one of the mothers started attending church. The vicar was able to support one family, as their son had to appear in court. A mess was made, but, in God's providence, a space was also made for people to hear about Jesus.

We moved into our vicarage in the month of February. As we got used to the neighbourhood, the weather started warming up. During this settling-in period, we began to realize that the churchyard seemed to host some rather dubious characters. It's only a small churchyard and open on three sides to local streets. We could see shifty people hanging about, usually in the afternoons as I headed off to collect the kids from school. Then, we started to recognize the car that these ill-looking folk were going up to, and notice some shady blokes whizzing by on bikes. Of course. It was the local drug dealers going about their business. Right in the heart of our community.

Over the course of the next few months, I got to know our local police officers rather better than I suspect is normal. And we called 999 three times on purpose and not just because a small child had got hold of my phone. I even berated one couple involved in a drug deal as I walked my daughter home from an after-school club.

As I gave the police more information and encouraged others to do the same, the police agreed to put up a CCTV camera opposite the churchyard. The activities of the dealers slowly halted. I'm sure the drugs are still around and that they're still being collected. In fact, my husband found a small stash recently when out with the youth group, hunting for a geocache (a hidden 'treasure' box located using a Satnav or GPS). But we don't see them much around here now.

Where did we see God's providence in all of this? It was in the development of local relationships with the neighbours. As I started my little war of reporting the dealers, I got to know my neighbours. We shared a common goal for our community, and so enjoyed a deepening of relationships that has carried on since the drug pushers moved away. Forging friendships over dates, descriptions and car number-plate details has led on to gospel partnerships. I can't look back exactly and say that the adventures with the drug dealers led to the salvation of an individual. But, in God's providence, that was a time when God's people were brought closer together and neighbourhood ties became more deeply interwoven.

Sometimes, we don't see how God's providence is working in the mess in our community. Broken relationships sometimes stay broken, and people reject our message of hope. But God is still the same, and his promises remain true. He works all things for the good of his people, so I can thank him in the mess and I can trust him with it.

Top tips: Some fun local community stuff

1. **Cake & Chat:** Many churches have toddler groups, which are great, but, once a mum no longer has toddlers and is still at home, a gap suddenly appears in the social calendar. Cake & Chat is our coffee morning, to which we've invited our school-gate contacts. Some toddlers come, but the table is a grown-up one. We put toys out, but the emphasis is on the mums and others who come. As well as home-made cake, we make cards and do other craft activities and sometimes have very short talks or testimonies. All you need are a church hall, a few toys and someone who'll bake. The baker doesn't even need to come to the group. In one church I attended, a kind lady who wasn't able to get out much baked in advance and froze her cakes. If your hall has more than one room, there is also the opportunity to run a Bible study of some sort alongside the consumption of comestibles. Ours is called Bible Bites and lasts just half an hour. Those of us not in the Bible study operate an informal crèche, meaning we watch any kids left behind. Each study is pretty standalone, so it doesn't matter how regularly people attend. Each bite of the Word will build them up, so, if attendance is messy or we're chatting anyway at Bible Bites time, we just leave it for a week. This is a slow-building work, seizing moments that are there and trusting God.

2. **DIY Holiday Club:** Our church is quite small. Running a holiday club is possible but it would be a big undertaking. However, the Cake & Chat gang like to meet in the holidays. So, we usually get together and provide an activity for older children who tag along, and sometimes a bit of Bible teaching too. This Bible teaching isn't as intensive as you'd provide in a club with lots of helpers, but it can be organized quickly and easily, and the gospel can be gossiped over cake.

3. **Tidying up:** Nearly every church has practical working parties, but, if we're doing the garden, it can take on a community fun day aspect. You'd be surprised at how many kids will come and want to have a go with the shears. This obviously works a lot better if your church is in a location where people can see what you're doing and join in.

4. **Event snaffling:** Is it Easter, Christmas, Halloween, a Jubilee or the Olympics? Do something – anything – and get people together.

5. **Make relationships:** Find local people to talk to regularly. Say 'Hello' to the people at your bus stop. Use the local shops – my husband and daughter got to know a lady at a nearby supermarket because they always went there at the same time every week. Or, have your hair cut at the same (local) place every time. I knew a group of four lads who shared a house, and they all had their hair cut by the same barber. This man had someone in his chair telling him about Jesus almost every week!

7. Messy meals

Steamed-up windows in a warm fuggy kitchen. An enticing aroma of roasting chicken with a hint of lemon, garlic and bay. A glass of sherry and some peanuts, perched on the worktop. Children happily playing a game of Cluedo in front of the fire. A vicar's wife frantically chopping carrots and calculating whether the already roasting potatoes will stretch to feed the extra people she invited. Suddenly, there's a dispute about who murdered whom in the billiards room. The sherry gets knocked over. The lunch guests ring the doorbell. The phone goes, and a dramatic pastoral crisis needing the vicar's immediate attention arises. The cat mews, signalling that her bowl is empty. Welcome to the vicarage at two o'clock on a Sunday afternoon. Will we eat before three? The answer is normally 'yes', give or take half an hour and some burnt roasties.

In our messy way, Sunday lunch is a regular fixture of the family and church routine. Most congregation members have joined us for a meal at one point or another. In the first year or so in the parish, we were slightly organized about it, to the point of going through the electoral roll. Now, we are a lot less focused and often invite our guests on a Sunday morning after church. Sharing a meal, gathering around a table to eat and talk, is a key part of life in our vicarage. This is one of the main ways in which Christians can show hospitality, an earnest expression of love which covers over sins. A roast lunch or a cup of tea and a biscuit can go a long way to building relationships, joining the body of Christ together and building new members into the church.

Our motivation comes from verses like this one in the New Testament: 'Above all, keep loving one another earnestly, since love covers a multitude of sins. Show hospitality to one another without grumbling' (1 Peter 4:8–9). Hospitality without grumbling is the aim, but preparing a meal for the family, let alone other people, can easily turn into a stressful burden. We have standards in our heads which involve ensuring that people not only eat enough, but also like our food, and even like the way it looks. We worry about inviting people over when yesterday's washing-up is still on the draining board. Can I offer them a cup of tea when they might have to clear themselves a space on the sofa? If I thought too much about the presentability of my house, I'd never invite anyone in. But the hospitality that we Christians are called to show to one another is not entertaining – it's a family welcome. Family get to see us in our mess, not in our tidy and organized state with everything hoovered and dusted. So, I don't need to grumble about tidying up. I can pray God's blessing on my welcome and invite them in.

Hospitality needn't even involve food. An invitation to join in – that's all hospitality is, and we can even offer it whether or not we have a kitchen and irrespective of the mess in our homes and lives. Hospitality builds the kingdom and reflects God's welcome to messy people. Let's work out how we can do all this without grumbling.

What is a meal?

A stolen piece of fruit, a famine, a hastily prepared meal of roast lamb, water and food miraculously provided, a man who comes eating and drinking, giving bread and wine to his friends, fish-and-bread lunches for many, a glorious wedding supper. From beginning to end, the Bible speaks about meals, about consuming food and drink. Hunger and thirst are some of the essentials of what it means to be human. These basic appetites define our days. They can bring joy or pain, can be marred by sin or can joyfully lift our hearts to God.

The Lord Jesus satisfies us in a similar manner to the way that eating and drinking do – he himself is the bread of life and he offers us water that means we will never thirst again. We eat bread and drink wine at the Lord's Supper as we meet with him in communion, remembering his body broken and blood shed for us. A meal satisfies us. A meal can point us to Christ. But, like our world and ourselves, our meals and our eating are also broken. From the toddler who throws her dish on the floor in a tantrum to the teenager arguing about breakfast cereal preferences: 'I'll only eat original Kellogg's, not this own-brand muck.' Illness and disease mar our meals: diabetes, anorexia and allergies can make eating alone, but especially eating together with others, a messy minefield of worries and anxiety. But still, we are called to offer hospitality, to share our lives and offer a welcome, to show the church and the world a glimpse of God's welcome and the rest that he offers to us. In this delightful, yet sometimes dangerous, part of our lives, God's grace and providence can help us navigate our way and bring glory to him.

Mini meals

A cup of tea and a Rich Tea finger. One of my favourite breaks. So, why not share it with someone else? Callers at the vicarage are almost always offered a cuppa. Sometimes we have a packet of Rich Tea fingers at the ready. Other times, there's a half-eaten packet with only soggy biscuits. Sorry. But a cup of tea and enough space on the cluttered dining table will do for a chat. It's a welcome. The offer of a hot drink indicates that I have space in my day. We only need half an hour to make a pot of tea and drink it, so the offer of tea (or coffee or herbal tea – we have a full menu in the vicarage) shows I have time. I can share a burden. I can point to the rest that Jesus offers to the weary. I can be available.

Sometimes, I need to be rather more organized about making time for people, or I need to visit and take the biscuits with me. It's OK to leave the laundry and the hoovering. Really. A youth centre I used

to visit had this motto painted across its wall: 'People Matter More Than Things'. It's a good reminder of God's priorities in the world. We are called to be a holy nation, a people for God's own possession. People come first with him, and so too we should be aiming to put them first.

Even taking time at work to get someone else a drink and sharing it with them is showing hospitality. Time and thoughtfulness, however brief and momentary, are the building blocks of relationships. At the heart of our God is the perfect relationship of the Trinity (God in three persons), and so our welcome and our hospitality will reflect God's welcome and build our relationships.

Over the years, I've had a variety of different prayer partners. Often, our prayer time has begun with a mini meal: a cup of tea, or (when I was younger and better at mornings) a breakfast before work. The time to drink tea gives you time to chat, but, once the tea is finished, it's time to pray.

Time and thoughtfulness, however brief and momentary, are the building blocks of relationships.

Kids just in from school always seem to be ravenous. So it's worth thinking of those ten minutes or so as an opportunity to practise hospitality with the family. There are, of course, times when I wave vaguely at the biscuit tin. But it's worth taking time to make something, or to sit down and chat and listen as we eat. It's always worth it in the end.

Rapid treats

If I've got someone round for a cuppa, I have a variety of snacks that I tend to offer. Sometimes, there are a few baking leftovers. But if there aren't any of those, here's what I tend to rustle up:

1. **Biscuits from the tin:** Obviously. It's not obligatory to serve something home-made. Or fancy.
2. **Cinnamon toast:** Mix 1 tablespoon granulated sugar with ¼ teaspoon cinnamon. Toast two slices of bread. Slather with butter and then the cinnamon/sugar mix. Pop under a hot grill for a few moments until the sugar bubbles. Eat immediately. You might like to keep a jar of cinnamon sugar to hand for regular cinnamon-toast sessions.

3. **Banana drop scones:** These take about five minutes to prepare and another five to cook. Good for anyone trying to avoid sugar, and they work very well with gluten-free flour too. The recipe is super easy, using measuring cups: ¾ cup (185 ml) self-raising flour (or plain with ½ tsp baking powder), 1 egg, ½ cup (125 ml) milk, 1 mashed banana. Mix egg and milk into flour, then add mashed banana. Fry gently in butter or oil. I like to make a batch of small drop-scone sized ones, but you could alternatively make a big one for breakfast. Also good with blueberries, or without the banana – you might want to add a couple of tablespoons of sugar in that case. Or drizzle with golden syrup. Makes twelve to fifteen of drop-scone size.

4. **Can-do cookies:** Great if you realize you have a bishop or a babysitter coming round and no biscuits in. They take about half an hour to make all in. You need 3 oz (85 g) margarine, 6 oz (170 g) sugar, 6 oz (170 g) self-raising flour (or 5 oz [140 g] self-raising flour and 1 oz [30 g] cocoa for chocolate cookie base), 4 oz (110 g) chocolate chips or raisins or similar. Cream butter and sugar, add flour (and cocoa if using) and egg, and finally the chocolate chips or whatever else you are putting in. I normally use a teaspoon to make about forty small biscuits on lined or greased baking trays. For bigger cookie sizes, use a soup spoon. Bake for 10–15 minutes at 180°C, Gas Mark 4. If your cookies came out too crispy for your preference, remember to bake them for a shorter time. The cookies will firm up on the baking tray after a few minutes.

Table meals

Gathering around a table to eat has been part of Christian routine since the Lord Jesus shared his life with his disciples, and especially since he instituted the Lord's Supper. We need not have cooked the meal ourselves; our table may be the floor or our laps, but eating a main meal with one another is a pattern we should try to retain in our timetable, however informal the culture. Whether it's weeknight teas or a Sunday lunch, it's good to think about how to eat well with others, when we've got little time or inclination and the kitchen is still full of last night's washing-up. I know there are occasions when we get totally inspired by the latest showing of *MasterChef* or a new Nigella recipe book and are dancing around the kitchen in our best apron. But they don't happen every night. Well, not in my house anyway.

It seems a bit sad, I know, but I usually have a recipe plan for the week, or at least for the busy nights. And I write it on the back of my shopping list before I head to the supermarket. At least, it means that I know I've got the key ingredients in. No good planning that green Thai curry, only to discover just as I've fried the chicken that I'm out of coconut milk. I used to plan most meals on the spur of the moment, but I can't get away with it any more, what with seven of us in the house and a tight early-evening schedule cluttered with swimming lessons, school-governor duties and church meetings. I also have a pretty set weekend menu which makes life easier. It's pasta for Saturday lunch, filled rolls for tea, roast Sunday lunch, and cheese and biscuits later. I don't have to think about it too much, but it's flexible enough not to get too dull. A bit of planning does make things a little less messy. At least, if I have a plan, I can do something else. If there's no menu, I've got nothing to start with at all.

In my head, I've set the places and everyone comes promptly to the table, the sink and drainer are clear, and there's calming classical music playing in the background. In reality, I've started cooking a bit late, none of the kids wants to leave the raucous game they're playing upstairs, the plates are cold, and I forgot to cook the broccoli. Since the kids were small, as you know, we've started our evening meal with a confession before giving thanks for the food. It seems a good time to confess – we've covered quite a lot of the day by then. And when even the production and serving of the meal are tainted with sin, it seems even more necessary.

Sunday lunch, that great British tradition, is our main meal for invitations. It's easily expandable, and nearly everyone is happy to eat a roast, or most of it. So, I roast something most Sundays, and a roast for six can easily become a roast for eight or ten, just with a few more vegetables and slightly smaller portions of meat. In an area that was more diary bound, I'm sure we'd schedule our Sunday lunch guests, but in our parish we're able to go more with the flow.

I always try to roast a largish joint, which we use for leftovers if it's not all consumed on the Sunday. And I make sure there are extra vegetables available. So, after church recently, I was able to invite a lady and her four kids to join us. I had a large gammon joint already boiled and ready to glaze and roast, and just needed to boil some extra potatoes and carrots when I got home. It was pretty chaotic, and pudding had to be improvised – ice cream with sauces and sprinkles, I think. But a meal provided messily is better than a meal not provided at all. And you can guarantee that everyone loves ice cream.

A few years ago, my older boy celebrated his birthday on a Sunday. We'd already planned a party for him at a local soft-play park, which

was scheduled for after school on the Monday. So, what about celebrations on his actual birthday?

To tell the truth, we'd not completely factored in his birthday when planning our Sunday. So we'd already invited three church members to lunch. They were an octogenarian chap and a retired couple in their seventies. The kids are used to having all sorts over for lunch, so they didn't notice that the people around the table were older than their grandparents.

Before lunch, they'd enjoyed showing their baby pictures to our friends, and the birthday boy had been demonstrating his new toys in the living room. Thankfully though, not the pogo stick. We all particularly enjoyed the new jokes from his Basil Brush joke book. A great birthday lunch, but not a neatly categorized one. A messy lunch with a rather random collection of people. This is true church: a meal with those who love Jesus, a sharing of lives and a connection between people brought together by God.

Top Sunday roast tips

1. **Gammon:** Boil it up before church (30 minutes per 500 g – you might need to get up quite early if you have a large joint and want to eat lunch at 1pm). Leave in the pot, and then glaze and roast it at 200°C for 30 minutes when you get home. I now boil it in water with an onion, cloves and bay leaves because I can then use the stock for lentil soup. If you boil in cola or cranberry juice, the joint is tasty, but you won't want to make lentil soup. Believe me, I've tried it, and it's strange. I glaze the fat by scoring it in a crisscross pattern, studding cloves in, then slathering it with mustard and sticking spoonfuls of brown sugar to the mustard. After Christmas, I use up cranberry sauce instead of the mustard-and-sugar combination. Because I usually serve gammon with mashed potato, expansion for extra guests is easy, as the mash is prepared after church. I've recently rediscovered how wonderful this is with cauliflower cheese on the side.

2. **Slow pork:** Shoulder is the best joint for slow roasting, although any joint will do. And it's also good value. Score the skin well and salt it thoroughly, getting salt right into the cuts. Then hot roast at 220°C for half an hour until the crackling has puffed up (before you leave). Cover with foil and cook for 2¼ hours per kilogram at 170°C. This should give you time to go to church if you have a decent size of joint – I normally use a 2 kg(ish) joint. When you get home, take the meat out, add some carrots, celery, leek, onions, bay leaves and garlic cloves in the bottom of the pan, then replace the meat and put back in the oven for another hour, uncovered. This will give you time to roast the potatoes. And if you add some water to the pan once the meat's ready to carve, simmer it for a couple of minutes and then push the veg and meat juices through a sieve, it makes the world's best gravy. Fact.

3. **Slow lamb:** I cook a browned shoulder of lamb in a roasting dish, on top of an already-boiling vegetable base of finely chopped onions, garlic, carrot and celery, together with about a glass of red wine, a few sprouts of rosemary and two to four tins of beans (usually cannellini, white haricot or borlotti) and about 2 litres of water. Covered with foil, it can be cooked slowly at 170°C for 4–5 hours. Plenty of time for church and refreshments afterwards. The beans are fabulous for lunch and as leftovers with crusty bread, or with pasta and any tiny shreds of lamb you might have left over. The lamb is great with mash or potatoes dauphinoise: potatoes sliced thinly, layered with a few herbs and a little garlic and baked in milk or cream in the same oven as the lamb for an hour or a little longer.

4. I generally use my oven timer for chicken and beef, as I've not yet developed a good slow-cooking recipe for either. Chicken can easily be expanded for extra after-church guests by bunging a pack (or two) of sausages in the oven when you get back. I usually keep some in the freezer, just in case.

Sunday lunch puddings without the faff

1. **Ice cream:** Everyone loves it. Sauces, sprinkles and sponge fingers can make it a bit fancier.

2. **Trifle:** Sponge fingers with a spot of sherry, some chopped fruit – tinned and/or fresh, custard or Angel Delight (butterscotch works brilliantly) and a tub of cream. Very quick to cobble together if you have the ingredients available.

3. **Eve's plum pudding:** Traditional Eve's pudding can be made using cooking apples, but I often use a 500 g punnet of those plums which are never very tasty raw. Cut each plum in half, removing the stones. Lay them round-side-up in a ceramic dish and sprinkle with sugar. Cover over with sponge mix made with 3 oz soft margarine creamed with 3 oz sugar and then 1 egg and 5 oz self-raising flour folded in. Bake at 180°C for 30–40 minutes until sponge is firm and golden in colour.

Church meals

A bring-and-share tea with quiche and cake, sausage rolls and ham sandwiches, samosas and Caribbean fried chicken (standards in a multicultural parish) and nothing green to be seen at all. You wouldn't say it was healthy eating, but it's always very *happy* eating, as the church family gets together at tables to eat and chat and laugh. Simple to organize: just add 'Bring something for lunch' onto the notice sheet, and there's the pleasing phenomenon of always having leftovers.

But sometimes, we make a right meal of eating together. A messy meal. We worry about whether there'll be enough to eat. Or we worry about the menu: getting it just right so that the foodie types in the congregation are impressed. We start thinking that it should be up to the standards that Mary Berry and Paul Hollywood would expect in the *Great British Bake Off*. Or even that we should be serving meals worthy of *MasterChef*.

Back to the New Testament: 'Let us consider how to stir up one another to love and good works, not neglecting to meet together, as is the habit of some, but encouraging one another, and all the more as you see the Day drawing near' (Hebrews 10:24–25). Remember that our meeting together is for the purpose of stirring one another up to love and good works, encouraging one another. It's not a cookery competition. If meeting and eating together is worth doing, it's worth doing with frozen pizzas and oven chips or a random selection of sandwiches, Scotch eggs and Bourbon biscuits. Let's meet together over food, and let the world out there worry about perfect presentation and gourmet treats.

Whether it's a church social or a wider invitation, it's all too easy for our meal planning to be burdened with professional expectations. We think people will be unimpressed with our rather ugly-looking home-cooked food, so we end up appointing a firm of caterers to handle the church lunch. Or, we send out exacting recipes for everyone to follow to the letter. Or, we surreptitiously bin dear Agatha's rather soggy-looking quiche. We regiment the family in a way that we would never do at home. At home, we accept the soggy quiche with gratitude. At home, we would happily be surprised that the delicious filling makes up for the damp pastry.

A church meal is a chance to demonstrate grace to one another and model it to our guests. The welcome shown by a church family is different from the welcome shown by the world. If a church meal is an opportunity with outsiders, we need to think carefully about every aspect of our eating together. We don't want to give anyone food poisoning, obviously, but neither do we want to pretend that church is a restaurant where all our cupcakes are matching, or where we are concerned about how we look rather than who we are.

Paul advises the Christians at Colossae to 'be wise in the way you act towards outsiders; make the most of every opportunity. Let your conversation be always full of grace, seasoned with salt, so that you may know how to answer everyone' (Colossians 4:5–6 NIV). So, we should be wise in the way we do meals for outsiders. If every meal is perfect, then there may be a danger of giving the misleading impression that the Christian community is *not* one of imperfection made perfect by the death of Jesus. Of course, we should make every effort to welcome others and feed them well. But, seemingly impossibly high standards can actually end up making people unwilling to join in. One friend attended a church where most members felt they didn't have enough time to make food of an acceptably high standard for church events. So, the congregation paid for catered meals. But the church then felt unfriendly to outsiders, and people in the congregation felt detached from one another. By outsourcing the making of food, the congregation had lost some of the ties that bind family together. So, for another event at that same church, my friend ended up handing out platters and asking people to fill them. The beauty of the arrangement was that people did not have to cook, but they had to choose some food. They gave something of themselves to the meal and therefore to all who ate. Just as the Lord Jesus gives himself to us as we eat his meal of bread and wine.

Beyond meals

Not every sharing of ourselves need involve food or even a cup of tea. It need not be in the home either. Creative hospitality can knit our church family together and welcome the outsider into a community that shares lives, including some of the more mundane and messy aspects. Meeting together can include walks in the park and trips to the zoo. We can meet together to watch telly or get on with a spot of weed-clearing in the back garden. We can talk while we wash the car; we can build the body of Christ over a bike repair or a visit to the cinema. Sometimes, that means planning and inviting, but, frankly, my best creative hospitality is usually spur-of-the-moment – seeing someone who can be invited and just asking.

We might also think about extending hospitality beyond the people we actually meet and know. There's the growing Christian witness of hospitality shown through the national network of foodbanks supported by the Trussell Trust. The foodbank in our town relies on regular donations of tins and packets by local churches. Our members have helped to serve food parcels to the clients, and many congregation members regularly bring food donations to church. People who are perhaps too frail to invite others over or involve themselves in church catering can contribute a tin of beans or a packet of chocolate digestives, thereby showing hospitality to some of the most vulnerable members of our community.

Grace for our meals; providence in our hospitality

Bless this bunch as they munch.

For what we are about to receive, may the Lord make us truly thankful.

All good gifts around us are sent from heaven above.
Then thank the Lord, O thank the Lord, for all his love.[1]

There is ample opportunity to get things wrong in our cooking, our serving of food, in our invitations and people's acceptance of them. That's a good reason to begin our meals with a prayer of thanks, often called 'grace'. But grace is more than just a prayer of thanks – it is food which God gives us and calls us to offer to others.

So, how can God's grace inform our meals and our hospitality? Gracious hospitality warmly invites people in without grumbling. How can I be filled with God's grace when the hungry hordes descend, and I've just dropped half the carrots on the floor and can't find where I put the gravy jug? Grace comes to us from Jesus, as I fix my eyes on him. If I remember the grace that has come to me, I can show grace to wailing kids or those guests I'd forgotten I'd invited. I can give thanks for salvation and dig out the crisps and offer a drink or a vegetable peeler.

Sharing a meal doesn't mean I have to do everything. A youth worker friend talks about getting young people from her church to fix their own food in her kitchen. Brave woman. But it's a time of grace for the teenagers. I can give and receive grace if I help in someone else's home or ask for it in mine.

Children grow if they're fed regularly. However, not every meal will be a special one: there'll sometimes be sausage, chips and beans or a frozen pizza. In the same way, our hospitality will grow our relationships. A special bit of hospitality from time to time may be remembered: maybe last year's Seder at church with fifty of us enjoying a feast of lamb and the re-enactment of Passover traditions. But other church meals are easily forgotten. That cup of coffee at the kitchen table isn't exactly memorable, nor is the shared soup on a winter Saturday. But the relationship is built. Bit by bit. The church has grown.

Even a meal badly done can be used by God to work his good. If the food runs out or we drop the pudding, we can still trust that God is able to use our mess for his purposes. We can work on showing the love that covers over a multitude of sins, including the sin of forgetting to bring a contribution to the bring-and-share lunch and the sin of putting too much chilli in the chicken curry. We can show hospitality without grumbling, trusting that God is completely in control of the fact that extra people have turned up needing feeding.

God's grace and his providence enable us joyfully to share the food he gives us with the people he has given us to love. We can show hospitality without grumbling as we remember that all-important welcome that Christ has won for us.

8. Messy celebrations

In a messy life, festive occasions spring upon you like a cat pouncing on a fledgling. There I am, minding my own business and suddenly – *ta dah!* – five birthdays and Easter and a bring-and-share lunch demand my attention. Now. No matter that I have Google calendar *and* a Filofax *and* reminders on my mobile phone *and* a snazzy box with special cards for birthday dates that was going to solve all the family birthday forgetfulness. Suddenly I have less than a week to go and I have Multiple Major Things to organize.

Meals have been covered already (in summary: frozen pizzas and takeaways are there for our de-stressing). But festive occasions, especially annual festivals, are times when I find I can take messiness to a whole new level. I have lists spinning through my head and stashed in different systems. I want to be creative but I can't find the space to think. So, how to cope amid the mayhem of expectations and desires to make the most of the rhythm of the year?

Annual festivals

If I was a proper Anglican, I'd know all the details of the church calendar, but the date of Trinity Sunday always escapes me. As it is, there does seem to be some rhythm to our year, what with Easter and Christmas and school terms. Retailers and the media increasingly tap into, or highlight, other seasonal reasons to shop, and our society grows small obscure festivals into must-celebrate larger ones. Although we're not fooled by the consumer-driven agenda, we've grown new family traditions to enable us to join in with our neighbours. So, for example, we now have some activities which we enjoy at Halloween, although we don't 'celebrate' it as such.

A regular round of festivals was a big part of the life of the people of Israel and Judah in the Old Testament – a time to rest and to gather together, and also a time to focus on a particular aspect of God's relationship with his people. In her book, *Treasuring God in Our Traditions*, Noël Piper calls regular God-oriented celebrations 'God's glue'. She says, 'Through them we learn about and recognize and experience the faithfulness of our God, who promises, "I will not leave you or forsake you" (Joshua 1:5)'.[1]

A regular round of celebrations can help us to hand on God's Word to the next generation and store it up in our own hearts. And we can do that despite our messy failings and a vagueness about the date of the harvest festival or Candlemas.

Messy Advent

You'll find a wonky stick with a few small twiggy branches stuck into a plastic tub on the island in our kitchen. The tub is wrapped in silver foil and filled with gravel we've scooped up from the drive. A child is suspending a fragile paper rainbow covered with shiny sweetie wrappers on one of the knobbly protrusions. It's 3 December, although probably not the third day in the official season of Advent, and we're putting up a Jesse Tree ornament in the vicarage. So far, we've managed all three Jesse Tree sessions, and the tree sports a big disc of gold and yellow card, reminding us of the creation of the world, and three apples which point to the time when Adam and Eve ate the fruit they had been forbidden to consume. I'm not sure why we have three apples in the collection that lives in the old chocolate tin. We seem to have acquired them anyhow, and it makes for three less fractious children on the day when we remember the sadness of the fall. Today, we are remembering Noah and his ark and God's promise never to flood the earth again.

The Jesse Tree has been a part of family Advent since our children were small. It has been a brilliant way to remember the story of God and his people, from creation to the birth of Christ. The tradition is to hang a different ornament on our bare twig from 1 December and have a Bible reading, with a few questions, which point to the coming of Christ. Each ornament reminds us of the Bible passage or a person who heralded Christ in the Old Testament. It's a visual Bible overview, helping kids (and grown-ups) see the big picture of God's salvation plan. (The series of readings and symbols that we use can be found at the back of the book.)

The beginning of December always seems like an oasis of calm, so we usually start pretty well. Then we are into a mêlée of plays and performances, emergency shopping and carol services. And there is no time to sit down for our Bible readings. But it's OK. Next year, we'll manage the reading for 16 December that we've missed, so we put double ornaments up on 17 December and keep going. It's not perfect, but it builds us up. It's better than not doing it. Always. We might not have the full overview all neat and tied up, but we've still seen some of God's story. So, it's worth doing.

It's worth doing in a less space-occupying way too. An outline of a tree taped to the fridge and a bunch of symbols printed off from the internet, or the Good Book Company's special *Jesse Tree Advent Calendar* are other ways you can achieve a rather lower-key version. And you can provide your own chocolate and not feel obliged to consume the rather cardboard-flavoured stuff that comes in calendars. Or use an Advent candle, burnt nightly – ours usually has twenty-four different names given to the Lord Jesus. A quick look at the Jesse Tree, however rudimentary, or at our half-burnt candle, and our minds are uplifted to God's purposes for Christmas, his Son and the incarnation, the salvation of the world, not the mess and darkness we bring to the season of light and life.

This verse from the Gospels takes on special meaning: 'In him was life, and the life was the light of men. The light shines in the darkness, and the darkness has not overcome it' (John 1:4–5).

Messy Christmas

On Christmas Day, as our church family is leaving the building and hurrying back to waiting families and their turkeys, a flood of people arrive and start setting up tables in the hall. It's the congregation of the Punjabi church who meet in our building each week. They are getting ready for their church family Christmas meal, attended by around fifty people. In the television series, *Rev*, a poignant Christmas special centred around the 'Waifs and Strays' Christmas Dinner'. Eating our Christmas meal with people we barely know, or who have chosen to come rather than been invited, is outside most of our comfort zones. How could we do Christmas like that? Unpredictably? Messily?

The temptation to hold a neat-and-perfect Christmas is a strong one. We are bombarded with adverts and articles detailing meals and pretty table decorations, present ideas and wrapping techniques. But how long do I want to spend preparing for Christmas? Does it need the 300 hours (thirty-eight days) reported by the media? Of course, I don't really have that sort of time to spare. So, the perfect Christmas is squeezed out and instead I will have the messy one. Because what I want to do is focus first and foremost on the Saviour and enjoy doing that with the family and with others.

We've been unable to visit family on Christmas Day since my husband was ordained, and they prefer not to travel at that busy time, so we've always invited neighbours to join us for our meal. We enjoy the fun of being with friends for food and crackers and silly hats, and for the *Abba* karaoke that has now become an after-lunch tradition. Eating with others means we can order a bigger turkey and go for all the trimmings. And we don't have to be consuming it until March. The British expectation of Christmas as a grand family reunion gives us the opportunity to open up our family to show God's welcome to others. This is what we should be doing in a society where lots of families are broken or struggling to get together – in our parish, many are thousands of miles away from family because they've moved to the UK from overseas. Rather than worrying about our comfort zones of tradition, how about offering instead God's comfort by inviting others in to share our day?

If we read Paul's prayer for the Christians at Thessalonika, and pray it for ourselves, we are reminded of God's eternal comfort to us and we can therefore bring that comfort to others: 'Now may our Lord Jesus Christ himself, and God our Father, who loved us and gave us eternal comfort and good hope through grace, comfort your hearts and establish them in every good work and word' (2 Thessalonians 2:16–17).

Christmas was pretty messy for the Lord Jesus – leaving the splendour of heaven to be born in a stable. The first Christmas was far from perfect. The accommodation was last-minute and not all that comfortable, and the event certainly didn't involve fancy table decorations and elaborate gravy recipes. So, a messy Christmas for us just reflects that first Christmas: a great wonder come to an imperfect world.

Messy New Year

I'm not very good at New Year resolutions. And if we've had visitors or attended a late-night celebration on New Year's Eve, I am sure to lack any moral fibre on 1 January.

But as the Christmas holidays finish, I try to turn to Don Whitney's ten helpful questions and write my answers so that I can reflect on them next New Year. If I was more organized, I'd probably do it more often than that. Perhaps this will happen at some point, but in the meantime some reflection is better than none, even if it's just once a year:

Ten Questions to Ask at the Start of a New Year or On Your Birthday
Once, when the people of God had become careless in their relationship with Him, the Lord rebuked them through the prophet Haggai. 'Consider your ways!' (Haggai 1:5) he declared, urging them to reflect on some of the things happening to them, and to evaluate their

slipshod spirituality in light of what God had told them. Even those most faithful to God occasionally need to pause and think about the direction of their lives. It's so easy to bump along from one busy week to another without ever stopping to ponder where we're going and where we should be going. The beginning of a new year is an ideal time to stop, look up, and get our bearings. To that end, here are some questions to ask prayerfully in the presence of God.

1. What's one thing you could do this year to increase your enjoyment of God?
2. What's the most humanly impossible thing you will ask God to do this year?
3. What's the single most important thing you could do to improve the quality of your family life this year?
4. In which spiritual discipline do you most want to make progress this year, and what will you do about it?
5. What is the single biggest time-waster in your life, and what will you do about it this year?
6. What is the most helpful new way you could strengthen your church?
7. For whose salvation will you pray most fervently this year?
8. What's the most important way you will, by God's grace, try to make this year different from last year?
9. What one thing could you do to improve your prayer life this year?
10. What single thing that you plan to do this year will matter most in ten years? In eternity?[2]

Messy Lent

What did you give up for Lent? Chocolate or alcohol? Twitter or carbs? Recent articles in both the *Daily Mail* and the *Guardian* discussed the enduring popularity (if you can call it that) of a season of fasting before Easter. That's when we can all gorge on booze and chocs while tweeting our way through a bag of battered chips. Or something like that. Lent has been observed since the early days of the church, although there is no certainty about how the tradition of a forty-day fast from Ash Wednesday to Easter Sunday (excluding Sundays) developed.

Lent can be good for us, and more than in a dieting sort of way. It can be a time to establish a helpful new habit or concentrate on expunging a bad one. Of course, I could do this at any time of year, but, since it's a time when the idea of self-discipline is specifically brought to my attention, it seems a bit stupid not to use the prompt. And of course, if I'm trying to practise some sort of self-discipline, this will be the time when my messiness rises to the fore, when I am totally incapable of achieving the goal I have set myself. Or I will find that the forgoing of coffee is replaced with tea, or the giving up of telly is replaced with Facebook.

In his letter to the Galatians, Paul describes the change brought by God's Spirit: 'But the fruit of the Spirit is love, joy, peace, patience, kindness, goodness, faithfulness, gentleness, self-control; against such things there is no law. And those who belong to Christ Jesus have crucified the flesh with its passions and desires' (Galatians 5:22–24).

My battle with the flesh can only be won by the Spirit's work, and I've always found that my flesh yields very slowly. Fruit doesn't appear instantly. A bud appears which flowers, is pollinated and then slowly grows. Spiritual fruit is the same. So, I often find I struggle to see growth or any progress and am tempted to give up. But forty days of Lent isn't long. If I've made a small change in my habits, even for a few days, that has brought me closer to the Lord or helped my family relationships, this has been worth doing. And next time, I'll manage it better. Or maybe I won't, but I know that, by his Spirit, God is changing me: 'And we all, with unveiled face, beholding the glory of the Lord, are being transformed into the same image from one degree of glory to another. For this comes from the Lord who is the Spirit' (2 Corinthians 3:18).

So, I enter Lent with high aims but with the cross firmly in my heart: the forgiveness that is available for failure and God's willingness to allow us to start afresh. Even if my failure seems trivial, I can start again and the slate is wiped clean. I can look at God's glory and remember that he is working in me.

Messy Easter

Midway through Lent, I need to remind myself to get some Easter eggs for the kids before all that's left are the Thomas the Tank Engine ones, which might not go down so well with my eleven-year-old daughter. I also need to dig out our Resurrection Egg set. This is an eggbox (surprisingly enough) of plastic eggs with small reminders of the Easter story hidden inside each one. We try, as with the Jesse Tree, to open one a day. And I have a stash of mini eggs to go with them to make it all extra special. This year, we started very late, so we did two or three a day. I have one friend who hangs her little tokens on an Easter tree. Another friend recently reduced the set to six (donkey, praying hands, crown of thorns, a small wooden cross, a stone and then the empty egg) and made take-home sets with families from her parish in a Messy Church event on Good Friday. And again, a sheet of paper on the fridge with a few symbols would serve just as well.

The Bible passages and story tokens I used for our Resurrection Eggs are listed below. Feel free to do it this way or completely differently:

Day 1: Matthew 26:6–13. Cotton wool ball soaked in perfume (not sure how Elizabeth Arden Green Tea compares to pure nard, but it was all I had).

Day 2: Matthew 26:14–16. Five-pence pieces for the silver.

Day 3: Matthew 21:1–11. Donkey or palm leaf. I used Playmobil pot plant pieces, but a piece of rosemary would do the job, or a paper leaf cut out.

Day 4: Matthew 26:26–29. Cup or bread. In ours, we have a Playmobil wine glass and a piece of bread.

Day 5: Luke 22:39–46, 54a. Praying hands or pipecleaner man. I stuck together some pink foam which I cut into the shape of praying hands. A little lurid in colour, unfortunately, but you get the idea.

Day 6: John 19:1–7. Purple cloth. The cloth in ours is maroon, but it was the best I could find.

Day 7: John 19:16–17. Cross. I made this by snipping off the bottom of one of the kids' palm crosses and sticking it together. A couple of matchsticks would work well too.

Day 8: John 19:18. Nails. Sourced from the vicarage tool cupboard.

Day 9: John 19:33–35. Spear. I used half a cocktail stick covered in silver foil.

Day 10: Matthew 27:57–60. Rock. Some gravel from the drive. Washed.

Day 11: Mark 16:1–3. Cinnamon/cloves/spices. Had plenty of these in the cupboard.

Day 12: John 20:1–8. And nothing in the egg! Easy peasy.

Messy All Hallows' Eve

It's 31 October. But we've not switched all the lights off at 4pm and hidden behind the sofa. We are redeeming Halloween, a festival growing in strength and popularity in the UK. Of course, I'd prefer it if there weren't a great big celebration of witches and ghouls. But, given that it's happening, we've decided that, if people are going to turn up at our door, we'll treat it as an opportunity to bless our neighbours and maybe get to know them a little better. You could see it as door-to-door evangelism. With the added benefit of people coming to *our* door, so we know they want to see us and won't slam the door in our faces. And with the totally in-the-back-of-the-net (for me anyway) benefit of mostly being able to sit on the sofa in front of the fire. Result.

Other churches have light parties or take kids door-to-door, giving out sweets instead of asking for them. In our old parish, there was a great community walk organized by a local church called 'Light up the Night'. People are partying, so we can take the opportunity to join in. Parties and walks can be yet more things to organize, so we like to stay home and wait for people to visit us.

Normally, we carve a couple of pumpkins, and the kids like to make the one with a scary grin. Into the second one we carve a flame, or a dove, or words: one year we had: 'Jesus is the Light of the World'. Then, we get in a big stash of sweeties and some Halloween tracts (the Good Book Company have a great selection) and make sure everyone knows we're going to be in and we invite them to call. Since my husband is Scottish, we also like to encourage callers to tell a little joke or sing a song on the doorstep in the Scots tradition of Halloween guising. But as kids often get stuck when put on the spot like that, we're happy to tell a joke to them instead. One of my sons has a great talent of knowing a joke for every occasion: why did the skeleton miss the Halloween party? He had no body to come with.

Some years, we've had a great time, with lots of visitors, while other years we've barely made a dent in the hoard of sweeties. But every year, local friends see our alternative pumpkin, receive a little gospel message and get to know us a bit better. The celebration of Halloween can seem to be against all that Christians are for, but we can bring light in the darkness, 'making the best use of the time' (Ephesians 5:16).

Messy assorted excuses

The Queen's Diamond Jubilee and the Olympics offered reasons to get the church family together and bless our community. In our small church, we struggle to hold many fancy events, but, with a bit of creativity, we manage a few fun ones. We hired a bouncy castle and barbecued a few burgers before trooping off all together to watch the Olympic Torch Relay that processed right down our high street. We announced a bring-and-share lunch for the Jubilee weekend the week before and only set up the tables after church. With a quiz and a happy mix of people, we laughed our way through enough food for all. Thankfully, it was quite unlike a festive lunch at one church I heard of recently where a newcomer without a ticket was turned away until the vicar's wife stepped up and offered to share her food.

We recently celebrated Rogation Sunday in our urban parish. Five weeks after Easter, this was traditionally a time when prayer would be offered for a successful harvest as the seeds were planted. This festival is also associated with 'beating the bounds': walking around the boundary of a parish to check boundary markers and ensure that land had not been encroached upon. So, we took the opportunity for a Sunday afternoon walk around the parish, stopping to pray at various points, including at the homes of some of our housebound parishioners.

If we look around us, we can usually find a reason to celebrate or get church and community together. And if there's no reason, we can always make one up. One friend has held an annual Family Olympics party at her home for some years. They invite a few families, run some silly games, and her husband gives a short gospel talk. Kids and adults enjoy the event, and neighbours are blessed.

My sister's house is small, but her friendship circle large. For her daughter's first birthday, she and her husband invited their friends to join them for a buggy walk round the local park. Then, they adjourned to a local pub for a birthday cake she'd baked and cups of tea and pints of beer. Church friends and baby group friends joined them too. A brilliantly creative approach to celebrating when home space is limited. A lovely way to bring church and community together.

Just before Christmas one year, when we lived in our first house in our first parish, we invited our church singing group to come along and sing carols for us. We asked our neighbours and friends, many of whom might not be prepared to come to a proper church service, to join us for mulled wine and mince pies. They could listen and sing if they liked, and then hear a three-minute talk on the meaning of Christmas. Friends who don't drink alcohol (or were driving) were served spiced cranapple, a convincing alternative to mulled wine:

Spiced cranapple

1 litre cranberry juice, 1 litre apple juice, 250 ml (1 cup) orange juice
5 cloves, 3–4 cinnamon sticks, 2 tbsp (or more to taste) sugar
1 orange, halved and sliced into rounds

> Combine all ingredients, bring to the boil and simmer for 15 minutes before serving. Works very well if brought to the boil and transferred to a vacuum flask.

Grace and providence in our celebrations

I always wish I was able to spend more time organizing big events and celebratory occasions. Most people love a good party, and you can get such a great buzz enjoying yourself with your church or community. However, in the day-to-day busyness of life, I don't always have the time to organize anything much. I can barely organize to get the kids out of the door on school mornings. And sometimes, that becomes the excuse to organize nothing. So, I want to press on and organize something, anything. Not to neglect meeting together (Hebrews 10:25), but to encourage my fellow saints, meet our neighbours and bring the light of the gospel. I want to help our children grow up seeing God's faithfulness through the familiarity of regular celebrations.

God's grace enables us to do something small and not be weighed down with guilt. We have a great God who takes a couple of fish and few loaves of bread and feeds a massive crowd (Matthew 14:19–21). A God who can take faith as small as a mustard seed and move mountains. He is able to do so much with so little. He wants us 'to will and to work for his good pleasure' (Philippians 2:13) as he works in us. He can use a celebration we think is meagre and bring about his good work. His providence can work great things, even through events we think unlovely or rather pathetic.

Let's celebrate, with church family, with our community, with friends and neighbours. Christians are Easter people, people with something to celebrate. There are all sorts of excuses to party and to build our church family and bless our neighbours. It doesn't need to be a big stress. We can party small or big and still bring blessing.

A messy life

Writing this book has been a messy process. When there are blank pages representing a manuscript waiting to be written, suddenly housework seems an attractive occupation. Then, a deadline approaches and it's takeaways for tea and everyone in emergency shirts as the laundry pile mounts. As I read these pages myself, I realize how far short I fall of the grace-filled, providence-trusting faith I've described. And so I pray:

A prayer for the messy

Loving Heavenly Father,
I am a mess. And yet,
Your power is made perfect in weakness.
May your power be made perfect in me.
Your grace is sufficient for me.
May I know that grace all day long.
All things work together for good,
for those who are called
according to your purpose.
May I trust your loving providence

through all life's ups and downs.
Lord, bless this mess:
this messy me, my messy life.
For you call me and you are faithful.
You will surely do it.

Appendix: Jesse Tree readings for Advent

There are twenty-five Advent readings here – starting from 1 December. Key readings are highlighted in bold, so, if time is limited and children are wriggly, just read that one verse. I have a sheet with all the single verses printed on it which I used to cut down on pauses when the kids were small. Now, we try to look up some of the passages in the Bible. Some of the symbols, for example star or angel, can be plundered from a box of Christmas decorations, and we made a bunch of others in the fuggy kitchen one Saturday afternoon, armed only with pipe-cleaners, some sheets of foam and coloured card, a few felt tips, some glue, scissors and sticky tape, and a roll of gold string to make the hanging loops. A colour printer and a bit of googling is another way of creating your symbols without too much stress. The Jesse Tree pattern below, including most of the questions, is largely taken from *Disciplines of a Godly Family* by Kent and Barbara Hughes.[1] There are loads of other Jesse Tree patterns which can be found online.

Day	Title	Bible	Questions	Symbol
1	Creation	**Genesis 1:1**; John 1:1–5	What did God create? Who was with God in the beginning? Who is the light of men and our light?	Sun
2	Sin	Genesis 3:1–10; **Isaiah 53:6**; Romans 5:8	Did Adam and Eve obey God? Why not? What is sin? Who sins? How did God show his love in spite of our sin?	Apple/Snake
3	Ark	Genesis 6:5–8; 7:17–23; **Romans 6:23**	Why did God send the flood? Was anyone saved besides those in the ark? What does everyone deserve? What is God's gift?	Ark/Rainbow
4	Abram	Genesis 12:1–7; **Genesis 12:3**	Why did Abram leave his home? What were God's promises to Abram? How did Abram respond to God's commands and promises?	Tent/Stars
5	Isaac	Genesis 22:1–13; **John 1:29**	What very hard thing did God tell Abraham to do? What does it mean to make a sacrifice? Has God asked you to do anything hard recently? Did Abraham obey God? Who is the sacrifice for your sins?	Lamb

Day	Title	Bible	Questions	Symbol
6	Jacob	Genesis 28:10–17; **Genesis 28:15**	What was Jacob's pillow for the night? What did Jacob see in his dream? What did God promise Jacob? Why did Jacob call the place of his dream an 'awesome' place?	Ladder
7	Joseph	Genesis 37:3–36; 50:18–21; **Romans 8:28**	How did Joseph's brothers feel about him? Why? What did they do? What did Joseph know about God and his plan that helped him to forgive his brothers? Is it easy or difficult to forgive someone?	Multicoloured coat
8	Moses	Exodus 20:1–20; 32:15–16; **Psalm 119:11**	What was written on the stone tablets? Who gave these laws to Moses? How many of the Ten Commandments can you remember? Why do God and our parents give us rules? What can we do with God's Word that will help keep us from sinning?	Tablets
9	Canaan	Numbers 13:1–2, 17–23, 27; **Psalm 103:2**	Would Canaan be a good land to live in? Why or why not? How did God want to bless the people of Israel? What are some of his blessings to you?	Grapes

Day	Title	Bible	Questions	Symbol
10	Ruth	Ruth 1:14–18; 2:4–18; 4:13–16; **Ruth 1:16**	Why do you think Ruth wanted to leave her homeland and family? What things had Boaz heard about Ruth? How did God reward Ruth?	Wheat
11	David	1 Samuel 17:1–9, 32–50; **Psalm 23:1**	What did Goliath look like? What did he do? Why did David fight Goliath? Do you think David felt afraid? Why or why not? Why did David win?	Sling
12	Josiah	2 Kings 22:11–13; 23:1–3; **Psalm 119:105**	What had happened to God's Word before Josiah's time? What did King Josiah do when he found the book? Why should we read the Bible?	Scroll
13	Stump of Jesse	Isaiah 11:1–5; **John 1:14**	How is Jesse (father of David) like a stump, and who is the new branch growing out of him? Who is full of grace, truth, wisdom, understanding, power, righteousness and faithfulness? How did Isaiah know about Jesus hundreds of years before he was born? How is Jesus God's living Word?	Tree stump with green leaf on top

Day	Title	Bible	Questions	Symbol
14	Lion and lamb	Isaiah 11:6–10; **Isaiah 11:6**	Will all the animals on earth be tame enough to stroke one day? Why will this happen? When will this happen?	Lion and lamb
15	Prince of Peace	Isaiah 9:6–7; **John 14:27**	What different names is Jesus called in these verses? In what ways does this world need a Prince of Peace? What things trouble you? Can Jesus bring peace to you?	Dove and crown
16	Shepherd	Isaiah 40:11; Psalm 23:1–2; **John 10:27**	How do shepherds care for their sheep? How are we like sheep? What must Jesus be like if he is our shepherd?	Shepherd's crook
17	Suffering Servant	Isaiah 53; John 10:14–15; **John 10:15**	What was God's plan for Jesus? Why is it important that Jesus died? Why was Jesus willing to die? What do you feel when you think about the cross?	Cross
18	New Covenant	Jeremiah 31:31–34; Hebrews 9:13–15; Acts 16:31; **Jeremiah 31:33**	What is a covenant? Do people always keep their promises? Has anyone ever broken a promise to you? Does God always keep his promises? What does God promise in these verses? How should we respond to these promises?	Heart

Day	Title	Bible	Questions	Symbol
19	Exile	Daniel 3:19–29; **Jeremiah 1:8**	What did Shadrach, Meshach and Abednego refuse to do? What punishment did Nebuchadnezzar order because of their refusal? How many men did the king see walking in the fire? How did God provide for Shadrach, Meshach and Abednego?	Fiery furnace
20	Return	Nehemiah 1:3; 2:17–18; 6:15–16; **Nehemiah 8:10**	What happened to the wall around Jerusalem after the Jews were captured and exiled in Babylon? Who enabled Nehemiah and the people to rebuild the wall? How did the surrounding people feel?	Wall/Brick
21	Bethlehem	Isaiah 7:14; **Micah 5:2;** Luke 2:1–7	What did the Old Testament prophets know ahead of time about Jesus' birth? How did they know? How long ahead of time did God know about Jesus' birth?	Bethlehem
22	Light of the World	Luke 1:26–28; 2:25–32; **John 8:12**	What good news did the angel Gabriel deliver to Mary? How did Mary react to this news? How did Gabriel describe Jesus? How did Simeon describe Jesus? How can you be a light for Jesus in the world?	Candle

Day	Title	Bible	Questions	Symbol
23	Jesus	Luke 2:1–7; John 3:16–17; **John 3:16**	Who sent Jesus into the world? Where did Jesus live before he came to earth? Why did Jesus come to earth? What does it mean to believe in Jesus?	Manger
24	Angels	Hebrews 1:14; Luke 2:8–20; Psalm 91:9–12; **Luke 2:14**	What was the angels' message to the shepherds? What different reactions did the shepherds have to the angels? What job did the angels do?	Angel
25	Star	Matthew 2:1–12; Revelation 22:16; **Matthew 2:10**	Who saw Jesus' star in the east and what did they want? Did King Herod want to worship Jesus? Where did the star come to rest? How is Jesus described in Revelation 22:16? How is Jesus like a star?	Star

Notes

Chapter 1 A perfect mess?

1. Bob Kauflin, 'Grace Unmeasured' © Sovereign Grace Praise (BMI).
   Used by permission.
2. John Piper, *Future Grace: The Purifying Power of the Promises of God*,
   rev. ed. (Multnomah Books, 2012), Introduction, 'Faith Is Profoundly
   and Pervasively Future-Orientated', para. 5, Kindle edition.
3. 'I am sure of this, that he who began a good work in you will bring it
   to completion at the day of Jesus Christ' (Philippians 1:6).
4. Thomas Watson, *A Body of Practical Divinity* (George and Robert King,
   1838), p. 47.

Chapter 2 Messy house

1. Thomas Watson, *A Body of Practical Divinity* (George and Robert King,
   1838), p. 122.

Chapter 3 Messy family

1. Phillip D. Jensen and Paul Grimmond, *The Archer and the Arrow*
   (Matthias Media, 2010), p. 22.
2. *Common Worship: Services and Prayers for the Church of England*
   (Archbishops' Council, 2000), p. 281.
3. Mission statement of The Round Church at St Andrew the Great,
   Cambridge, cited in Christopher Ash, Mary Davis and Bob White
   (eds.), *Persistently Preaching Christ: Fifty Years of Bible Ministry in a
   Cambridge Church* (Mentor, 2012), p. 36.

4. Tim Chester, *You Can Change: God's Transforming Power for Our Sinful Behaviour and Negative Emotions* (IVP, 2008), p. 88.

5. Thomas Boston, 'Of the Providence of God', in *An Illustration of the Doctrines of the Christian Religion with Respect to Faith and Practice*, vol. 1 (George and Robert King, 1848), p. 193.

Chapter 4 Messy kids

1. Matthew Henry, *Commentary on the Whole Bible* (1710), Psalm 127.

2. Susan E. Beck, Gloria Oostema (illustrator), *God Loves Me Bible* (Candle Books, 2006).

3. L. J. Sattgast, Toni Goffe (illustrator), *The Rhyme Bible Storybook for Toddlers* (Zonderkidz, 1999).

4. Catherine DeVries, Kelly Pulley (illustrator), *The Beginner's Bible for Toddlers* (Candle Books, 2008).

5. Catherine DeVries, *The Beginner's Bible: Timeless Children's Stories* (Candle Books, 2005).

6. David Helm, *The Big Picture Story Bible* (Crossway Books, 2010).

7. Cindy Kenney, Big Idea Design, *Veggie Tales Bible Storybook: With Scripture from the NIrV* (Zonderkidz, 2006).

8. Linda Sattgast, *The Rhyme Bible Storybook* (Zonderkidz, 2000).

9. Bob Hartman and Krisztina Kállai Nagy, *The Lion Storyteller Bible* (Lion Children's, 2008).

10. *International Children's Bible* (Authentic, 2001).

11. Sally Lloyd-Jones, Jago (illustrator), *The Jesus Storybook Bible: Every Story Whispers His Name* (Zondervan, 2012).

12. Eugene H. Peterson, *My First Message* (NavPress, 2007).

13. Marty Machowski, A. E. Macha (illustrator), *The Gospel Story Bible: Discovering Jesus in the Old and New Testaments* (New Growth Press, 2011).

14. Doug Mauss, Sergio Cariello (illustrator), *The Action Bible: God's Redemptive Story* (David C. Cook, 2010).

15. Stuart Townend, 'How Deep the Father's Love for Us' © 1995 Thankyou Music.

16. Keith Getty, Stuart Townend, 'In Christ Alone' © 2001 Kingsway Thankyou Music.

17. Paul David Tripp, *Age of Opportunity: A Biblical Guide to Parenting Teens* (Presbyterian and Reformed Publishing Co., 1997, 2001), p. 105.
18. Ebenezer Erskine, 'A Discourse on the Throne of Grace', in *The Whole Works of the Late Rev. Mr. Ebenezer Erskine, Minister of the Gospel at Stirling*, vol. 1 (1798), p. 244.

Chapter 5 Messy church
1. From the blog Sussex Parson: Marc Lloyd's Miscellanies (http://marclloyd.blogspot.co.uk/2013/02/a-typical-service.html).
2. For more information about this organization founded by Lucy Moore, see www.messychurch.org.uk.
3. Mark Ashton, 'Eight Convictions about the Local Church', in Christopher Ash, Mary Davis and Bob White (eds.), *Persistently Preaching Christ: Fifty Years of Bible Ministry in a Cambridge Church* (Mentor, 2012), p. 17.

Chapter 7 Messy meals
1. A selection of modern and traditional Christian grace prayers said before meals. The verse is taken from the popular harvest hymn 'We Plough the Fields and Scatter' (1861).

Chapter 8 Messy celebrations
1. Noël Piper, *Treasuring God in Our Traditions* (Crossway Books, 2003), p. 36.
2. From http://biblicalspirituality.org/newyear.html.

Appendix: Jesse Tree readings for Advent
1. Kent and Barbara Hughes, *Disciplines of a Godly Family* (Crossway Books, 2004), pp. 162–187.

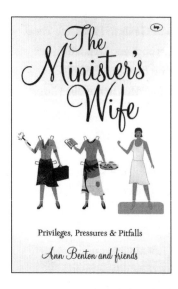

The Minister's Wife
Privileges, pressures and pitfalls
Ann Benton and friends

ISBN: 978-1-84474-556-2
208 pages, paperback

The Minister's Wife will show you how to make perfect cupcakes, turn out well-groomed children every Sunday morning and rise to the lofty heights where criticism cannot reach. In short, you will quickly become the model minister's wife.

Unfortunately not. However, what this book will do for you is help you to look honestly at the privileges and problems of the manse and the rectory. It will free you up to become the best you can be, unencumbered by nagging concerns about issues that don't really matter.

You are first and foremost a minister's wife before God. What a privilege! This book looks also at the minister's wife's responsibility to her husband and children, as well as to her wider family. It looks at the often-overlooked perks of the job, as well as at thorny issues such as boundaries, forgiveness and forbearance.

Here you will find wisdom from eight women, distilled for a wider audience. It will be an honest friend to the minister's wife, whether experienced or just starting out.